The Book of Healing

Sandra Nešić
(Angel S)

Sandra Nešić
The Book of Healing

Translation: Jernej Theuerschuh
Cover, layout, and illustration design: Lana Stojan Zavašnik and freepik
Cover photography: pixabay
Photography of the Author: Nataša Kralj

ISBN: 978-1-83556-440-0   Hardback
ISBN: 978-1-83556-441-7   eBook
ISBN: 978-1-83556-442-4   Paperback

Book Design by HMDPublishing.com

Ljubljana, June 2025

Original title: Zdravilna knjiga

Table of Contents

To all the people on Earth.
Let LOVE be the guide on the path of life.
I wish this from the bottom of my heart.
For the Earth and all of us.

Acknowledgements

With love and reverence,

I bow in gratitude to every soul who has, knowingly or unknowingly, touched my path and left their imprint on this journey of inner awakening. This book was not created alone. It was held, nurtured, and uplifted by both visible hands and invisible grace.

To God—my first and eternal guide—thank You for entrusting me with this message, for leading me gently yet powerfully, and for whispering when I forgot how to listen. This book is, above all, a humble offering of the love You have poured through me, and a fulfillment of my quiet desire to someday write a book.

To Saša —my deepest thanks. Without your steadfast belief in me and in the purpose of this book, *Zdravilna knjiga – The Book of Healing*, would have remained a dream. Your loyalty, your strength, and the way you quietly held the net while I dared to fly… I will never forget. You carried this book with me to its very birth.

To Mirjam, who saw the light in this work and, with a touch of divine timing, connected me with the person who would help bring it into the English language. Truly, I believe it was Divine wisdom that sent you both my way.

To Jernej, thank you for your generous heart and for lending your voice to mine through translation. This English edition exists because of your dedication, clarity, and spirit. You didn't just translate a book—you helped write a piece of history.

To Lana —one of the greatest blessings on this journey. You were heaven-sent. Your creative fire, grace, and generosity colored every corner of this book—from editing and illustrations to the breathtaking cover design. You always responded to my requests with kindness and enthusiasm. Most importantly, you designed the book cover, which continues to delight me every time I see it. Thank you for saying yes to our Amazonian dream.

To my dear friend and photographer, Nataša —thank you for always seeing me through the lens of love. Thank you for capturing my essence with the camera, even though I put you to the test with my requests. The photo on this cover carries your warmth and artistry.

To my beloved children, Iva and Davor—thank you for walking beside me all these years with patience, respect, and quiet strength. Iva, I know this book asked more from you than most will ever see. Only God and I know the full measure of what this offering means—for us, and for the world.

To Aleksander —thank you for holding my faith when mine ran thin. You never wavered, not once. You saw the power of this book from the start, and in doing so, you helped me see it too.

To Sanja and Manja —thank you, soul sisters, for walking this spiritual path with me in such harmony. Your presence, your wisdom, and your unwavering support have anchored me. Thank you for helping bring this book into the world with love and for organizing my first book presentation — an unforgettable moment in my life.

To Aljaž and Anja —thank you for your contributions to the original Slovene edition of this work. Every detail mattered.

And to my beloved mother, who is no longer here to hold this book in her hands—I carry your love in every word. May this book be a living tribute to your spirit. Your light walks with me still.

To everyone who held space for this book to be born — thank you. You are part of its healing story.

With all my heart,

Sandra Angela Nešić

Introduction

"I, Sandra, am an angel incarnate."

This is a message; I have been tasked to write by the dictate of God. While writing this book, it funnily enough felt more like being "God's secretary", as I am merely writing down the channeled divine messages and teachings I receive by the grace of God.

I'm protected by Jesus himself. Jesus guides me, and Jesus shows me the path. I am a light in this world, channeling all of the good and positive vibrations alongside love and its beautiful associations. I am a being of love. I have been given immeasurable beauty and the heavenly opportunity to spread this beauty to the world further. With this book, I wish to bring to the world the message of God, who is ever present, not just in me but in all creation. I am his channel, his medium, so that I can write down all his messages brought down from the divine and angelic sphere. Each time I receive a message, I tell you, my dear friends, I write it down exactly as received. Through this process, a book of messages will be formed. A book of messages that will spread love like a letter to a dearest friend.

Through this book, love will spread. He named this book The Book of Love. A book of healing, whose every word will spread love, awareness of self, and understanding of the oneness of the universe. All of this - through love.

God, in his wisdom, has assigned Jesus himself as my guardian. That I can connect to our heavenly leadership fills my heart with such tremendous joy. It is my wish that this process of healing connects you to the divine as well. There is no greater love, beauty, or greater remedy for the soul than to be connected with divine leadership. That is the purpose of this book.

Word of the Author

This book contains 60 stories and teachings that I transferred to the pages during channeling. Before every channel, a short message was communicated to me that was not directly connected to the chapter following the thought. Perhaps some might find the language used by God to be a little alien and strange because the way God speaks is very honest and direct, but always loving. The text is written exactly as I have received it. You will see that God likes using metaphors for the ingredients of life and key life situations. He always lovingly addresses me as Angel. While his vocabulary is indeed a little bit different than what we're used to, I like it. I like it when he uses the word nonbeauty for something ugly, and for something dirty, he says that it is not clean (it is "unclean", "not white"). He speaks about sickness as the absence of health. Everything he says, he says in the spirit of love and the good of all of us and this little Earth. I believe that some of you will catch yourself when you don't understand something. But don't fret, don't get stuck, and continue reading, in time, you will understand.

When reading this book, you will actually realize (and feel) that the entire thread of this whole book is just one thing – LOVE. God says that this book is also healing. While reading, you will receive healing by studying how you think and mostly by studying your emotions, through the use of cleaner, better, and more beautiful feelings. I wish that you would open up so much and feel the plenty that the universe is saving for us in all areas of our incarnated life.

At the end of this book, you will also find the message of the angels. I connected with them as well so they could tell me the message they have for all of us on this little Earth.

I wish you a happy journey through the pages of this book!

Sandra.

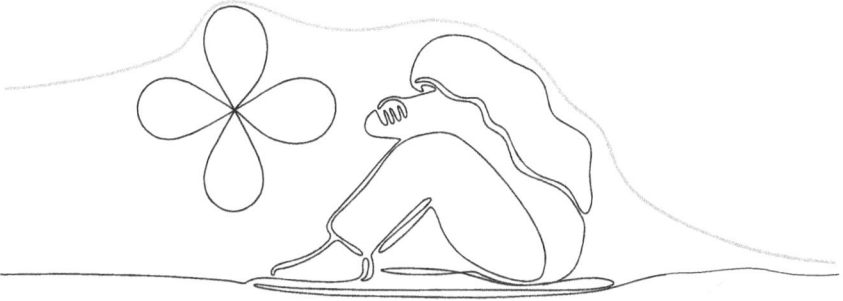

"The light conditions the loudness of your heart and love you have for yourself."

Ljubljana, 7th September 2019

1st message: FEAR AND LOVE

This is a book of love and about love. This is the book of the great creation. Our love is present everywhere; we must only look for it to find it, and once it's found, it's ours and unforgettable.

Life contains two things: **fear** and **love**. Fear follows us through our insecurities, shifting blame to others, intimidation of others for our own gains, and loss of will to live. When life loses its meaning, we sway like a branch of a dying tree. This is what we become when we submit to all the fears ever present in all aspects of our lives. All the while, our human body persistently takes it all and bends, while our soul suffers, cries, and yearns for more. It yearns for the other side, the side of light, the side we rarely set foot on. However, once truly awakened, we can throw down the excess layers and, through the soul channel, return to the side of light and live once more.

What is life? A collection of events that lead us into fear, despair, vanity, idleness, and non-beauty, a collection of negative events that suffocate the soul. Or it can be eternal love. Ever-present Love, veiled behind the curtain, which we need only to unveil. The curtain is thin, white, see-through, and sways like a mighty flag in the wind. Friend, come and remove the veil, expel your fear, and make the step to the other side!

What will you find there? Light. Glory. You. Your soul. The Angels. Me. God. A place of divine radiant beauty, that shines in the light of every person, a shine that sometimes hides and distances itself. Where does it go? A place unknown.

What is your message here, God? That I am sometimes wounded when I watch unhappy souls hurting themselves and, in so doing, hurting me. You become yourself once fear and doubt are left behind, and you feel your true self. You become me. You deserve all the peace, freedom, and love of this world. Within a sunflower is a seed that is just like us. Aware of beauty and the great beyond, we cannot see when we are sad. We must leave behind this consciousness that isn't, as it is not free, and its cost is steep.

What, my friend, do you wish to hear from me, God? Is it not joy? I can give you joy, but listen first. History is written in books, yet no one has grasped what we must do to step onto the side of light with joy, happiness, and honesty, and so we must discover the path to the perfection of our being. We are living beings that rise and rise like a bird soaring toward the sky.

Why do people wonder what they must do when it is so easy? While it is easy to leave this place called Earth, suffering blinds the senses and clouds your mind. All the joys, all the knowledge of angelic beings, God, and life on earth, are changing constantly and growing bigger and mightier with every leap forward. The vibration is increasing, but it is not high enough yet. We give too little love to people. Love is everywhere, we must only find and pick it up.

Friends, read these lines, this is my message.

God.

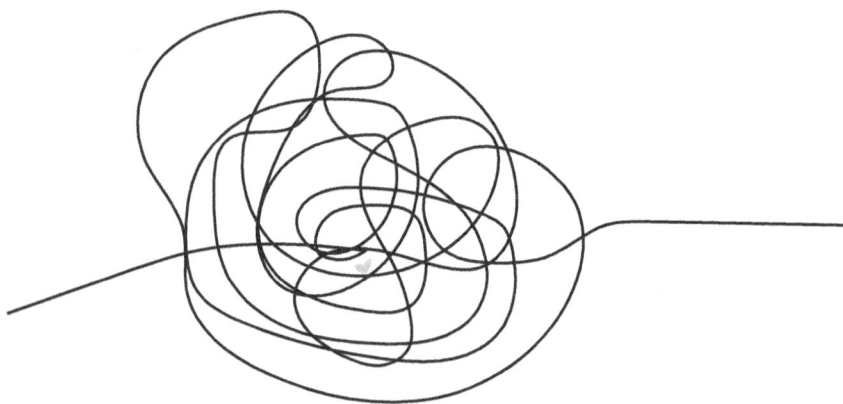

"Your holidays and special days, spend with those
you love and cherish."

Ljubljana, 8th September 2019

2nd message: HATE

Dear Sandra,

My love works through you. What message should we share with the world in this book? Today, we will talk about hate. Hate leads us nowhere. Friends love each other, as hate is not a good emotion; it does not have the pleasant fragrance of angels. Can you, at this moment, smell the fragrance of your angels? That is not hate, that is love. Yet everyday people feel hate: hate towards others, themselves, their surroundings, their job which they hate, their coworkers, their arms and legs, their painful losses, their inner self, and their heritage, which didn't bless them with the beauty and love of joy, their properties, and imperfections, their stories which they reveal to the world on social media…

Sandra, our love, my light, tell them this:

Stop loving just yourself and your ego, as it is destroying you. Stop smoking, drinking, finding excuses within others, and stop hanging out with others like yourself, which drag you down to the bottom. Start writing a beautiful story – a story to enrich yourself. Leave your painful heart on the platter of someone you love, forgive yourself all of your troubles, go into nature, create and find your shelter within the giant with the giant heart, who will only fill the world with love. Beyond yourself, find great happiness, which will not dampen your fortune… Find yourself a partner who will make you happy.

Love is so great and powerful. Hate is not! Hate undermines every single person and every single soul. Drink water and tea, which do not dampen your soul, but embolden it and help it grow and purify. The well is full. Full of clean water, and you must take it with a great big bowl from deep within. From the depths. The depths of the water that will cleanse you.

Why do people hate? Because they hate themselves, and outside of themselves, everything is different. Beyond yourself is love, pure, as from a well. Will they grab it? What do you think? They must, or they will spend their life traveling the paths they do not like.

Can you hear that sound? The sound of the unhappy? It makes it hard for me to look at them when I see how they bat their eyelashes when on the verge of crying. They need to stop Sandra! They need to stop and figure it out for themselves - only pure love, the pure love of the well.

The well is the source of love. Can you imagine the deepest well where the water is love? Pure love. When you grab the water from it every day, you clean your soul as you would with the purest love. That is how you heal. Heal the hate. Friends, love is disappearing. Disappearing from your lives. This is not poetry, my friends, this is pure love. I am not speaking of fairy tales, but telling a story. Write your story, but only one that will make you happy. What do you think will make you happy? Money, mistrust, not beautiful relationships, misfortune, and hate? Never! Only the purest love from the well will bring you happiness.

Grab it every day, and your bowl should be golden and the biggest in the world. You will drink the golden water from the golden well – pure, golden love.

Love each other, my friends, and let go of the hate. Abandon it and throw it away. Hand your hate to me, my angels, and Rafael, so you can hear my voice, which is always there. Come, drop the emotion of hate into the energy of the universe, and let it wilt there! Why is this hard to do? It is not! Let go of your doubts, which feed your hate for yourself and others. Repent each day, in the morning, repent each hour, repent, and look at the beautiful new light.

Why does hate kill? Because it kills your soul and kills your body. Your body and soul begin to decay when you hate. They decay into the smallest subatomic particles. Why? Because hate is the ugliest emotion, which weakens every atom of your body, mind, and soul, which is now crying and not rejoicing with you. When you hate, a black incomprehensible destructive chemical reaction is destroying every atom, every single piece of your soul and body and is leading you to make incomprehensible choices and actions. Thus, you become unreasonable as the delusions of your mind take hold.

Be reasonable and enter the well. Within it use the golden bowl and take hold of the angelic love and love yourself. Love your mind and body, every atom and cell of your body and mind. Love your fellow man, cat, dog, your boss, your fellow prisoners if you're in prison, your superior or underling, and the residence where you live and work.

Love yourself and leave your ego at the bottom, where it will die! Listen to yourself, listen to the sound, and hear the decisions of your inner voice.

LOVE. Just that.

I love you,

Your God.

"Share your love through your smiles, feelings of happiness, longing, joyousness, and a life of radiant white."

3rd message: MUSIC HEALS

My Sandra,

My angel, I am with you. Now tell the world what I wish to tell you. Music, music heals. Friends, listen to your favorite song, play it, and be enraptured by it as if you are there with the music in the ether.

What does music say to each person? That he is synchronous, that he is in harmony as a melody. A melody of a great eternal bell that rings. Ding, ding, ding… What drives the bell? To be heard far and wide, and for people to attune to the chime. Just put your cell phone into the most hidden corner and listen to the melody. Melody from the radio, instrument, computer with a speaker, or without — whichever you prefer as you listen to the harmony of music. What does it make you feel? What goes through your head as you absorb the melody? Are you overwhelmed by the sound, or are you attempting to relax and feel good? Try to embody the music in yourself. What guides you? What kind of thought guides you when you are listening to your favorite melody and you have your dog or cat or turtle, or fish in an aquarium beside you?

Do you relax? Are your muscles tense, your mind calmed, and limitlessly beautiful? Listen to this, as it is then that you hear yourself. Your inner self, your soul essence, that which you cannot see in yourself. Do you get chills when you hear your favorite song? What about a song from your younger years when you danced with your favorite chosen or your classmate? Do you get chills when you hear music so beautiful you just want to dance? Do you remember your thoughts as you sang your favorite song in your younger years? What do you think about it all?

Were you driving in your car with your significant other listening to your favorite song, singing it out loud, and feeling the wind in your hair? What do the memories stir within you? Beautiful memories. Memories of better days, youthful days when you were happy. Relive it – what are you waiting for?! It is this feeling that will raise your vibration and bring you joy. Limitless joy reaching the sky. It is when you feel that feeling that you are in contact with me, with God, with the divine, and with yourself. As the bliss of a nursing child. The child is then in a blessed state.

But what is the blessed state for you?

The calmest feeling is when you are in contact with yourself. No stress, no noise. Just you, me, and you again. Nothing. Nothing else. What else do you need to feel this way? Nothing and no one. Just yourself. You and only you.

This is where the beauty lies, in the disconnect from everything, when you forget everything, and are calm and receptive to only yourself. It doesn't get better than that. That is also the only way you can achieve something in your life. When you are calm. When you are in this state, you can snap your fingers and get everything you wish. Bullshit you will exclaim, that isn't true… But it is! It is! Why?

Because when your point of vibration is highest, you attract all that is good. Try it! Do you think you can manifest a car if you spend all your time crying, being fearful of not having anything, becoming angry, screaming, losing your temper, playing games, and then going: "Hey, I want a car, can I get one?" Absolutely not! Why?

Because your point of vibration is at zero, at zero point, because of which you are - pardon my expression - emitting a signal of shit, and shit attracts more shit. That is how it is in this universe and with all the people on this planet.

So, what are we going to do? We will take the radio and listen to our favorite radio station, hearing the songs, which will raise us up, heighten our vibration as we dance, hum a song, and – get this – feel good! This good, **joyous,** rapturous feeling will please you the most. We will emit this vibration, and then we will attract true wonders into our lives. Do this several times a day and you will see. What does it cost you? Nothing. Absolutely nothing. Just a few more happy feelings, dancing, humming, and loving yourself. That is life, my darlings, not crying, indulging in fear, fearing death, pain, or anything else…

With you,

Your God.

"Do not tune another when you are out of tune."

4ᵗʰ message: EVERYONE CAN HAVE EVERYTHING

I truly wish for everyone's happiness and full lives filled with plenty. I cannot get past the fact that people are living in poverty, with nothing to buy bread, clothes or other basic necessities of life.

What is it within people that drives them to not have enough for basic things when there is everything in plenty? I would like to know, and so would like you to give this message to the world. What to do when you cannot afford bread or pay the bills? Do you give up or fight and drive the story of abundance onward? What do we have to do so we can buy a piece of bread and some meat at the store? What about a bigger thing, which costs a lot? Is this difficult to do? No! Take it to the bank – there is plenty everywhere. It is accessible and within reach. Not just to the wealthy but to all of you! Then why do people live in poverty? Why can they not afford the basics, be it milk, bread, meat, or a car? It doesn't matter if it's bread, milk, salami, or a luxury bag.

To some, the bag is just pocket change, and to others, some meat is a world of plenty. Is this not how it should be? I am telling you, everyone can have everything. But what is everything? Everything that the human mind can imagine.

Love is the guiding principle of this world, and it does not know the limitations that people have in their heads.

1. First, listen to yourself and your own thoughts. Are you aware that people often do not even want what they wish for? They say one thing and wish for another.

2. Often, people will cry after things, instead of being grateful for what they have. They make fun of that which they do not have, and because of that, they do not have it.

3. It is too late to cry after the rain. When we are vibrating on the lowest frequency all the time, we only attract that, which only exists on the lower frequency: doubt, despair, unhappiness, sadness, crying, and fear, fear, fear. This prevents us from obtaining what we wish.

4. Are our wishes in line with what we live? If we live in poverty, it is poverty that we will get, own, and feel.

5. Go into nature and ask yourself, how it works, and how all the animal species survive in nature. Do animals also fight for basic things, like food? No! Because they instinctively know they will get what they wish for.

6. What do you think you have accomplished in life? Did the limitless line of infinite possibilities reach you yet? No? Then continue with what you are doing now, and you will not find plenty. It did? Then continue on your path, and you will receive plenty.

I, God, promise you that you will have everything you wish, if you choose it, feel it, and allow it – if you invite plenty into your life. Have you ever manifested? If you have not, then based on what was said, ask yourself why not. If you have, you are winners, and continue on your path, as I do not care whether you wish to manifest a piece of cheese or an expensive automobile.

I must now take you to the golden chambers of the most beautiful villas, where riches, peace, and happiness rain. Here, plenty lives in all its beauty. And who has plenty? The wealthy. The wealthy attract everything, because they *think wealthy*. They think they have everything not because they were born with everything, but because they wished for it, wanted it, and worked on allowing the manifestation to occur. It is in vain to think swords will rain from the sky if the weather is nice. But we can think, to make it rain, when we wish for rain, as the weather knows, where to strike and where, so people will have water, courage, happiness, and life…

I must now also tell you the following tale:

"There was a village in which an old man lived with a barefoot brother. The latter was always poor, and the old man was rich. But one day, the old man sent his barefoot brother to a watchmaker to fix his watch and get 5 gold coins for his troubles. The barefoot brother declined, saying he couldn't go to the watchmaker as he had other things to do. The old man told his brother, "Would you not take the watch to the watchmaker, even if I give you 5 gold coins?" The barefoot brother replied: "No, I can't because I'm going to a wedding tomorrow and need to clean my shoes. I can't go to the watchmaker. Maybe tomorrow." The old man kindly told his brother that tomorrow would be too late, as he needed his watch. But the barefoot brother still complained that he couldn't go because he was busy."

Do you see? The barefoot brother had, despite his poverty, rather cleaned his shoes at home, instead of earning 5 gold coins for doing just a bit of work. But why? Because he would rather stay poor than have plenty reach him. It did not reach him because:

- Of his thinking about the money;

- Excuses that he will not be able to make it to the wedding for fear of losing too much time at the watchmaker;

- His faithlessness about having more money;

- His unwillingness to make the money come to him.

That is how it is with people to this day. Listen to what you say, what you think, what you wish, and feel, and you will know why you do or do not live in plenty.

Your God.

"How much time do you need to offer your love to others
and yourself? You don't have enough time.
If you wait, your time will be gone."

Ljubljana, 9th September 2019

5th message: THIS BOOK BEARS A HEALING RECORD

Dearest Sandra,

Our angel, today, we will write down why this is a book of healing and why it carries a healing record within. We could call it *The Book of Healing* or *The Book of Love*. Souls, which work in the context of this book, are approaching divine leadership beyond this book. Perhaps at first, people will frantically wonder how a book can heal when it is just words on paper. Yet it is. Letters, words, entire sentences, and the entire text can heal, because the book is written in the spirit of God, through the eye of God. My healing energies flow through every single letter. Within it is energy. Within it is love. Within it are teachings. Teachings about love, which never wane. Every person should read it. Every person will while reading the lines in this book become a tiny bit more enlightened, pure, healthy, and light. Your hand is merely writing. You are my channel. Like the channels in Venice. As you can see, I also make a little joke at times. Forget your phone right now and focus on writing the book. I still guide your writing instrument, your pen. Keep writing, keep writing, it will stop ringing (while channeling, I left the phone on in the other room). Did you see it? The phone quieted down. What will people think when they read this book? Ah, another book on top of all the others! But no, this is not true! This is your mother (who is quite persistently calling me on the phone). Leave her ring. She wants to see you, to talk to you (and sure enough, her name shows up on the phone after I finish my channeling). People think that they can only affect others with

18

a word, sight, or sound. But no, it is not just our hearing, sight, and taste that we can hear, see, and taste. It is the energy that we feel that moves us. Your letters will move the world.

This book is something special. It is the beginning of a new chapter of life for each person who wishes to learn more and achieve enlightenment. So read it, my dear friends! The lesson I'm bringing forth through Sandra's mighty pen is powerful. Read every line, think, absorb, and pay attention to what you're feeling. Is it joy, happiness, or delight? Is it fear, doubt, and insecurity? Are you perhaps deep in thought as you read these lines, and possibly scared – have you asked yourself how you feel?

Ask yourself how you feel! I know you are **already** feeling good. It will be best to think about the healing process in your mind and body, to think about the new you. Are you thinking about it? Yes. Because every word I'm sharing is a healing lesson. Because it truly heals. It is not a medicine, yet it heals. Because it is bright and it is light. Everything made of light heals. As you are reading this, a light, a shine begins to dwell within you. As you read this, within yourself, a healing that does not come from medicine is taking place inside you. This is a spiritual healing that is not physical, but emotional and spiritual.

So, dear readers, read this book, which will begin the healing and transfer my shine, light, and love through Sandra's pen to you.

I love you.

Your God.

"You are a gem. It is within you.
Find it and polish it to perfection."

Ljubljana, 10th September 2019

6th message: **WRITE A BEAUTIFUL STORY**

My dearest Sandra,

What I will tell you today is truly precious. Precious for every single person, because the life people enjoy on earth is precious. Do you not see what advantage you were given when you were born and embodied as a physical creature, that originates from the divine and is the work of the divine? This is your work, your being, which must bring the divine energy even further. Further into life. But life is not a fairytale for most of you. Most of you do not live in plenty, and some even in poverty: with no home, no food, no children, nothing... Was this why we sent you to the face of the earth? No, my dear souls, we sent you so you can enjoy the love of paradise, all the plenty of this world. It can all be yours. So why isn't it? Because you do not allow my dear friends. Your thoughts, your restricted thoughts, are sometimes so clogged up and inactive that you are unable to bring anything good into your life, into your life experience. Relax your muscles, look into the sun, go out into nature, drink clean water, eat food that doesn't poison you, and be happy. Why can't you be happy? You always have two paths you can take: to be happy or to be unhappy. Choose the path of happiness, choose yourself. In this way, you will be receptive to writing, designing, creating, and every eternal moment that will carry you into divinity. Here is that which brings you plenty, happiness, spirituality, an active life filled with angels' hugs and beautiful loving experiences, and not in fear, despair, uncertain dreams, and moments.

Your moment is today. Be aware that only at this moment does the story you're writing happen. So write it beautifully. Use a beautiful writing style and paper that will be smooth, shiny, bright, light… Douse yourself with love, and in all the moments of weakness, throw your fears away. Stay away from the life that isn't yours and weakens you.

Let me tell you a story:

"With the years, the girl became increasingly wrinkled and old. Mother asked her: "What will you do with your wrinkles and your age?" The daughter replied: "Nothing, mother, I will live with them and love them. Because that is the only way I can love myself, love others, love you, and be joyous in life. Why would I be upset about my wrinkles? They remind me of my maturity, the beauty of life in all its shine, and all its glory. And I wish to be beautiful with my wrinkles. Within them, I see the path I walked in life." "Do you see my wrinkles as beautiful as well?" the mother asked. "Of course! Always because I look at you with the eyes of love, and beauty shines out from your eyes, and because of that, I love you the most in this world," her daughter said sincerely."

How often have you thought about your blemishes and wrinkles in this way? I thought about them daily, and not just about the wrinkles, but about all of life. What good will money do if you do not love or respect yourself, if you do not love and respect others? But you can have money because **you love** yourself. When you love yourself, everything loves to come into your life. Even money, when that one is not even the most important. What's important, my friends, is love. It is the most important. To love yourself so you can love others, and so allow other people to love you. It is then that plenty will flow into your human life.

I love you.

Your God.

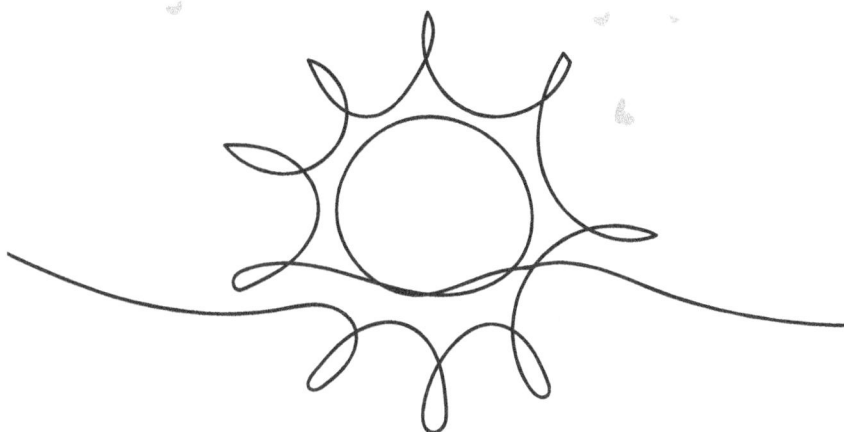

"A sharp corner will not let you pass.
But you can avoid it and find the round one.
That one will give you a smile on your face. "

7th message: OPEN YOURSELF TOWARDS THE LIGHT

Dearest Sandra,

Start writing. There is nothing that makes you more human than your head. Writing a book is difficult for some who choose to do so and for others not. Listen now, why it's difficult for some: because they are not open and receptive to the words that would otherwise excite them, and so in the future, they will choose a different path.

But what of those who do not feel it to be difficult or hard? They look positively at the world, with open eyes, pupils wide, and open arms, marching confidently and mightily on their path, just as a giant. You can do this, too, my friends. Write the book effortlessly and without difficulty. Why would you make your writing difficult? There is no need for that pen yourself up, open up your chakras, and allow them to work in the magnificent light and let them spin for you, accept, and also give light for you. Relax, and guess what my next words to you will be. There is no mighty person who does not love or relax. One who does not love or relax is not mighty. They are a creation of their miserable heart, captured in the dark. This cannot continue.

Mightiness does not come from material gains, it comes from the divine. The part that you, my friends, do not see. That is why you **must open your *feeling heart*:** make it beat in the divine rhythm. Only the piece of the divine **slowly opens towards the light**.

What is light? Beautiful, invisible, energy of pure divine, divine that heals. It gives you energy to live, to receive, and when received, to work to become a state of love and mighty divinity. Then you become a heart that beats in the rhythm of the divine. The light you must learn to accept it. Accept it through your spiritual channels, we call chakras. To receive the light, open your chakras.

Write, laugh, smile, dress well, and feel all the good, and you will feel the light. Let the feeling of boundless happiness and joy lead you back towards the light. But how? By opening your heart, smiling, feeling all the joy and plenty, and going to the heavenly space, a space that gives you plenty, peace, and beauty.

Your God.

"There always comes a point when you realize you're not alone."

8th message: A WHITE HEART DOES NOT JUDGE

The rules of the game are known in life. People love to comment about others, insult them, gossip about them, and mention things about them that are not important and do not connect to our continued happiness. We cannot ignore the fact that these actions destroy happiness and joy, and sour the relationships between ourselves. We must remain open to the beautiful, happy, and joyous moments. When moments come when we want to talk about the acts of others, we should bite our tongues, sing a song, and instead be beautiful. It is not in our nature to judge. **Judgements are not divine.** Judgments are not the work of angels but the devil. They come from the depths of the ego and not our soul.

Let us take in the beautiful thoughts of others and not judge everything and everyone. It is not our job to think about others, their opinions of us, or their actions. Let us think clearly with a head that is not for sale. Divine thoughts are big; they are the thoughts of a giant. Not just a tall man, but a giant, with a giant heart. The sanguine heart of such a giant beats hard and fast and is drenched with love. All the threads, veins, and parts of the heart of the giant are soaked with the substance we call love. Is this substance red? I do not know. But I think it is as white as light. But the color doesn't really matter here. You may imagine red because the heart is red, but love is white.

White is the color of light, the color of giants. It shines and is hidden within is the healing whiteness of the white light. That is why its essence is healthy, strong, and clean – it is the essence of the heart.

The essence of the thread that crisscrosses this pure, beautiful white heart. **A heart** like this **does not judge**, does not gossip, does not raise its hand upon another, and no one, it only gives. Gives and gives. Beauty, warmth, and all that love can give.

Why? Because this symbol pleases **love**. Love of **cleanliness, beauty, grace, and goodness**. It is the symbol of love.

We draw a heart like this:

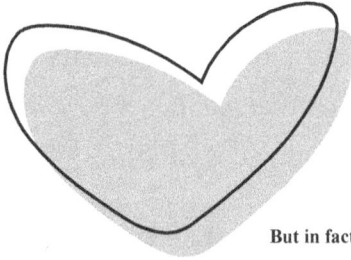

But in fact it looks more like this:

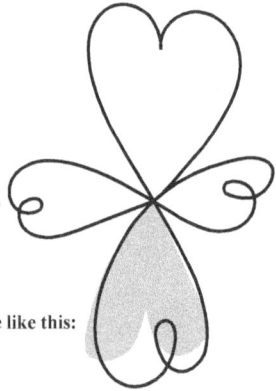

Most people who think that they do not have a lot of money, happiness, humor, beauty, or grace do not fit this symbol. Yet we must only open our hearts. To possess a white heart. Just as a laundry basket filled with white garments and white things, we can wash and wash and it will never stain. But when it does, we wash it. That is how even the white of the heart gets stained. Do you understand me? When the laundry gets dirty, we wash it. That is how we must wash our own white heart. We clean it of the non-white dirt and dark.

But how do we do this? We must become aware of ourselves

and our situation, and ask ourselves what we intend to do. Are we going to hold our heads in our hands and cry, or go write another chapter in this book? We will write the new chapter with a clean white pen, a pen the color of a white dove. We will write the chapter of the happy moment, which will help us raise up happiness, vibration, and awaken the white feelings. How will we achieve this and keep our white emotions? By petting a dog, or laughing at the neighbor who cut his grass too short, or dug a flower hole for his wife too deep. By going out with someone who will make us laugh and live, by grabbing a coffee, or by letting the sun's rays warm and caress our cheeks. By reading a good book or hugging someone close to us. By dancing in the rain or sun, by licking the chocolate of our fingers and so, even farting when we want to (God gives a mischievous grin).

Understanding is a great thing. It is based on the fact that people know everything and understand everything already when they are newly born. At that point, we know and understand a thing like we have never seen or heard about it before. We just know. We know we cannot leave again and go amongst the clouds once more, we know that here we have a purpose and here we may return again.

Is this hard to accept? When we know our time is limited. We cannot run away and say: "Hey, I'm not doing this anymore!" That is when you stand and say: "You are God, you have God within you, so you can have anything and make it happen! Even the whiteness of the heart."

Your God.

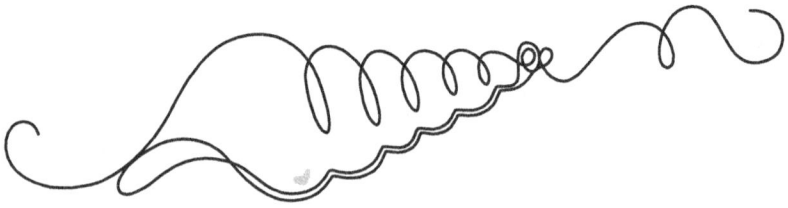

"Your qualities are your virtues, seek them in yourself not others."

9th message: WHAT IS YOUR VIBRATION? IS IT LOW OR HIGH...

Dear Sandra,

Our angel, you are like the sea, which waves between the worlds and rocks. Hitting the rocks, going back and forth, here and there, and again you disappear, God knows where.

Our emotions are a reflection of our mindfulness. Our system of leadership, operated by emotions, expresses our thoughts very well. When we are confused, afraid, and scared, we feel a sea of bad emotions. We are like the sea I mentioned earlier, we are thrown here and there, and we are like the water that runs down channeled creeks. That is how our emotions look when we experience negative ones.

Thoughts are just the totality of the sensations that we feel. Our life is full of crazy emotions that we sense in our everyday feelings. When we release the weight of the burden of our emotions to a level we call the ultimate, then we know bad things are about to happen. We feel the amplified fear, and the solution to the crisis can be difficult. When we make a step forward, we start to walk the path which rises up a bit above, but the rise is still not yet enough as the rise starts to sink. To feel is to be like the tide, going up and down, from the state of ultimate to the state of ecstasy. Ecstasy is the extra special feeling on the other side, which is something special and which we want to always shake off of us, due to shame, fear, and primitive patterns within ourselves. Let us not punish ourselves for feeling ecstasy. It is but the tip of the mountain of ice. Instead, let us try to climb off the mountain and increase the heat by stepping down into the lower parts. Through ways like these, we can increase our comfort and improve our emotions.

We cannot outfox our emotions. Emotions are ours and are a part of us. We carry them in the core of our body and soul. Once they go after us – and they go after us most of the time – we should stop and ask ourselves, what the emotions are attempting to say, what are they trying to convey to us.

Are we smart enough to outfox them and play Old Maid? No. We can never outfox our emotions. They are an expression of us, our minds, our worlds. These emotions can only be controlled by attempting to vibrate differently. Vibrations are a reflection of our emotional tides and our feelings. Whether we are up or down. Where would you want to stay for most of your time? Most of the time, people spend below, yet wish they were above. Can you imagine this world if we were all up on the higher vibrations? That would be one happy, fulfilled, inspiring, beautiful, perfect, and most experiential planet Earth, which would positively glow from positive vibrations and positive energy.

Sadly, that is not reality. All people vibrate in different ways, on different levels. Most vibrate low, many average; however, more and more are trying to increase the world's vibration. But is it hard? No, it's not. You must only decide how you will vibrate. Are you up or *below*? If I were in your position, I would wish to be up above, as it is full of beauty, plenty, and abundance. Plenty abounds up there.

Everything is enough. Beautiful relationships, money, love, wonderful relationships with your partner, beautiful gatherings, everything… You decide where you will be.

The lower vibration is boring, and nothing is going on, and if you ask me the souls below are dead. Abundance has been lost and there is a lack of everything. So why my friends, would you insist on staying on the lower vibration when it is better up high?

Let me draw it out:

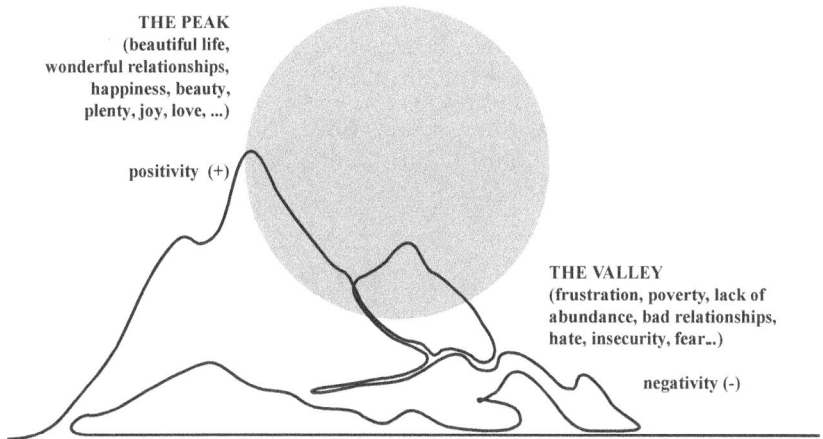

THE PEAK
(beautiful life, wonderful relationships, happiness, beauty, plenty, joy, love, ...)

positivity (+)

THE VALLEY
(frustration, poverty, lack of abundance, bad relationships, hate, insecurity, fear...)

negativity (-)

That is how this works. You are either up above or down below. How are you vibrating? You can feel it. Your feelings can tell you whether you are on a higher or lower vibration. Do you think you are on a high vibration when you are scared? Never. You are only there when you are vibrating with love.

Your God.

"Can you see the world around yourself? See it? Good.
Through which glasses are you looking at it? Pink or gray?"

11th September 2019

10th message: FEELINGS AND EMOTIONS

My dear artist,

Today we will write about **emotions** and **feelings**, of beautiful words and the greatest sin that can happen to a man – the confirming ("amen") love, and about death (God speaks of this in the next messages).

Are feelings like the tide? Yes. Feelings are like the tides of our hearts. It endlessly ripples like the sea. The sea was once rough and once at peace. Once living in the high tide and then the low tide. We most often hear it when the sea is rough. That is when the emotions come out in the form of an unwanted suit we wish to take off and replace. This is the tide we wish to stop and snuff out. But an emotion cannot snuff itself out without our help. Without our thoughts and our minds. Let's give it a song, *a nice outfit* and the biggest drag so the tide goes out and the heart waves down to a lower level, to a slower rhythm, which will then pass.

Is it God's purpose for our body to feel these beautiful emotions or the other cumbersome, rock-like, relentless emotions? Certainly not the latter one. I, God, wish only for the emotions of a person next to quite a low tide, which arouses the heart and keeps it healthy, and wish for healthy thoughts that flow and know the way to go.

Your job and our job are not to suffer, to behave like a hurricane, to cast judgment on others and yourselves, but to shine in all your bright white light. The light of the world shines eternally, you merely do not wish to see it. Go on, look how close it is.

Your job is to see it. Give it a chance, not the pain. The pain drains you and makes you sick. Tomorrow I will talk about sickness, well, maybe a bit before. What is sickness? Do you deserve it? No, most definitely not.

Emotions. Let us return to emotions. What do they say they reflect? Your emotions, physical, and mental state, which you project outward. Waves of emotions cannot be well described but felt. This is the feeling that the person waves inside themselves. These high and low tides are sometimes immeasurable. It changes so fast from being impossible and windy and relentless, to other times being so loving.

Why am I talking about feelings? Because these are the only things important in your body, and they tell you everything. Emotions are the work of the mind; feelings are the work of the soul. Listen to your soul's feelings. They always tell you how you feel, and you must be careful as they tell you how and what to do next.

What then do we do when our feelings fool us? When it's not yours, when it does not love you, when you wish to push it aside because you hate it? It's then you most want to jump into the sea, the tide of the sea to snuff it out. But do not snuff it out, but sense it, close your eyes, relax, go outside into nature, sit down and tell yourself in a calm mind:

What is it you wish to tell me, feeling?
What do I do with you?
What do I do to get rid of you?

Should I continue to fight you and your power, or should I make peace with myself? What will you tell me in this moment? Should I leave and quit, or face you?

TELL ME FEELING!
I AM HERE,
I WISH OUT OF THIS SITUATION
Talk to me!

And the feeling answers: "I'm afraid, I don't feel good, I'm hungry as a wolf because you don't feed me with real food, you feed this body with this weird, unhealthy slop, which paralyzes me, and I don't sleep well, and wake up constantly. I am anxious and depressed, I just want to feel good." Did you now hear your answer, my mind, my body? Did you hear it? That is what I have to tell you.

Go forward and feel it, sense it, and start to feel better because you know what to do, because you know, you know what you can do, because you've faced your precious feeling, which is your guide and is showing you the path forward. It is your leader. It tells you what you are, what you are feeling, and how to move forward if you only listen to it. And when you listen to it and hear it, what do you do then, friend?

Then you look inside yourself, take a deep breath, close your eyes, and ask in a small, beautiful prayer that you feel better, that you start to feel the purest tiniest bit better with your senses prepared for the better times, the happier feelings, that will invigorate your body. As if awakening from your most beautiful dream.

Do you know the feeling when you awaken from your most beautiful dream? That, my dear friends, is how you must feel. As a dreamer awakened by the greatest treasure of light, the greatest happiness, all the grace of this world, and the warmth of the light of the heart. The heart trembles, calms down, and starts the blood flowing into the other, prettier, most beautiful side of life, which we call love. And when you, my friend, feel love, you will be in a state where your feelings will go from a state of vanity and ugliness to a better, more beautiful state of empathy, your love. Then you will feel the shine of the light inside your soul and the most beautiful meaning of life.

When this happens, go and do the things that you love doing. After that, you will have ideas that will resonate with you, and you will be as productive as you have ever been, as your soul will be in tune, your mind at peace, and you will be feeling good. That is when miracles happen, that is when people invent great things. Scientists' great new discoveries, experiments, inventions, and artists' greatest masterpieces. That is when I, God, am at work in all my shine and glory. There is no misery, fear, or doubt then. That is when people feel only themselves and eternal love.

So, what do we hear when we are out of tune? We hear the banging of the heart, the heart ripples like the waves of the ocean, thrashes, fights, and wishes to become in tune again, and when we do tune in, it wants to stay connected to our beautiful mind and clean, pure body. That is when the soul is free inside a clear mind capable of anything. Do not let it off its reins, dear friends, for the heart will once again be swept into the tide, the time, and rocking of the shoals. Of course, you do not want this. And I do not want this, and so is the reason for this message.

Your God.

"The difference between you people is only in the way you are in tune with yourself."

11th message: WHAT DREAM DID YOU HAVE TODAY?

Dear Sandra,

Let's talk about **dreams**. Dreams are a big part of our lives and indicate what we think, speak, and feel throughout the day. Do you remember your dreams when you wake up?

Usually, my friends you do not remember. Why exactly do you not remember them? Because you do not know what or even if you were dreaming, as your mind is not present enough to transfer these dreams into reality, and your life. You don't remember your dreams because your nervous system did not write them down into the notepad in your mind. It happens that we step on what we've just dreamed. We simply do not remember anymore. But what should we do so that we can really remember these dreams in the morning when we wake up. Come, let us rein in our minds and ask it, what did we dream about today? It might give it a try, and remember, it might not. It depends on the intensity of your dreams, the intensity of your dancing in the face of divinity while your mind was not around. What you wish to accomplish with these dreams is your problem. It can be a lot, and it can be nothing. But I am telling you that your dreams are a great indicator of your subconscious and your daily thoughts, so do not neglect them. Oftentimes, they will tell you about a scenario you are wondering about, but not a scenario you want. They will tell you what you think about it so that you might ask more. So before you sleep, always close your eyes, stop for a bit, calm yourself, retreat into yourself, and ask what you wish to know about your dream.

Tell your mind, body, and soul to dream an intensive dream, and tell it to recognize those dreams in the morning, and you will remember them. It will make you feel good when you get an answer to a question you asked before you slept. This answer will tell you a lot, to do this or that, in this way or that, it will tell you what to do in the future, and maybe show what awaits on the path ahead… Perhaps the dream will be unclear, but do not worry, as the important thing is that you remember it and write it down. Write them down in a dream journal. Once you read them, you will find a lot more answers than before.

Why write down your dreams? By doing this, you're transferring your mind, your daily and future activities, on paper. Your dreams are important, as they reflect **yourself**! Your dreams reflect yourself, my dear friends! They are very important. Do not drive them away. They are an indicator of yourself and your physical life. Why neglect them when they have so much to tell?

Instead of relying on your psychics and fortune tellers (well, they need to make some money too), turn to your dreams instead. Your dreams will not always be pretty. Not even in your dreams can you imagine that. Your dreams will always be an indicator of the path and everything you think you must do, of what awaits you in life. They will even show which path to take, what to think about it, and in general, what's going on in your life. Do not neglect them.

This collection of events in the invisible state of sleep is very valuable to you. I'm telling you to ask and write about your dreams. This is your guidance, your path, and your life.

Your God.

"You are still alive if you are aware of your own happiness.
A soul that is dead is not."

12th message: DEATH – THE BUTTERFLY'S METAMORPHOSIS INTO THE WHITE LIGHT

Dear Sandra,

My angel, your mission is to help people and help spread my teachings. Let your word be available to people all over the world. This mission and these messages I give into your hands. You are like my white dove carrying my words into the world.

This time we will talk of the passing on of living creatures, we will talk of **death**. This should become something sacred and not taboo. Let the death of each person be something that entirely receives and takes the spirit and the soul into the great beyond. My message to you, my friends, is this: do not fear death. Do not be afraid to die. That is just the human perspective on those who must return home. Return to the angels and the creator, to me, to the other side. Metaphysical experts would call this a spiritual transformation. A butterfly that flies and is no longer being hunted. It just flies and flies, where no one will stop it. A white butterfly beyond a great, beautiful meadow is carried to the great beyond by the wind. Is there anything more beautiful for the human eye to see and mind to grasp than the transformation from white wings to a beautiful heaven? When he dies, a person transforms into a butterfly that gets picked up by the biggest breath and is blown out into the great beyond.

It is wrong to be afraid of what will happen when you die. Do not be afraid, you must just let go. Let yourself go into the flow that takes you to the whiteness, to the light, back to the bright white darling beings. That light is my home. No more human soul, just a beautiful white light–energy which overtakes you. The body falls away into a thousand pieces and a million particles; it falls away to dust, while your soul moves and, like a butterfly, transforms into its own shining home. This home is a universal eternity and is home to all the souls that live on this light side. The home is eternal, limitless, and ever-present. It does not move, it merely transfers the soul into another life in which you might again meet your soul mates and twin flames.

That is why you should not be afraid of death. It is something only the body and mind experience, but not the soul. You see, the soul is immortal, eternal, and so does not feel it. It only feels the body as it falls off like a coat. The butterfly then transforms into the white light. Can you imagine what you become when you die?

Here, let me draw it for you:

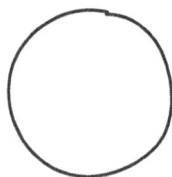

THE TRANSFORMATION

THE BODY, that
withers away

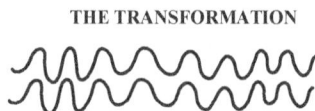

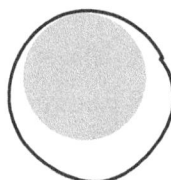

GOD (= HOME),
this is the soul in the white light, surrounded by
fellow soul-mates.
This is home or the "devine sphere"
that is never-ending,
it does not wane, it does not end and is ever present.

Why are you people afraid to die? Because you think that death hurts. But when the body transforms, it merely does this:

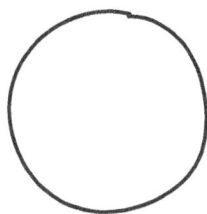

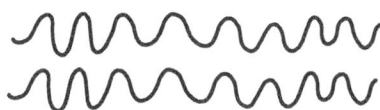

HOME
where there is
no pain

BODY

The transformation of the soul is not painful. You are already halfway home at that point. Can you imagine how beautiful it is when your footsteps cross the threshold of your wonderful home, where it's warm and bright, and you're greeted by a warm bed, your loved ones, and everything you love? What does home mean to you? A home is divine; it is something the soul loves. It is home there.

Once both legs cross the threshold, this is what it looks:

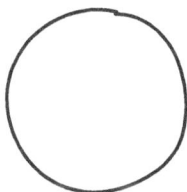

BEAUTIFUL,
positive, harmonic and
joyous feeling,

because in a moment you KNOW
you are home

And the soul is home again, able to feel the most beautiful feeling that a soul can know. My friends do not think that crossing the threshold (death) is painful. That is something that hurts you and that you must fear. Fear is an illusion, a cliché, and a horrible emotion in people's heads that drags them to the bottom. Dying, my friends, is just a phase where the soul crosses the threshold of home and transforms into a divine being on the other side.

Dear metaphysics, you will understand me as you know that dying is not something terrifying or traumatic, but something divine and beautiful, which brings us back home into the company of other divine souls already waiting, and those yet to come.

Death is not bleeding, it is not disease, and it is not painful, but a liberating salvation of a soul going into the great beyond without its physical coat. As people need to take off their coats, jackets, and heavy clothes in the summer, so too a soul must discard its body (literally undressing the soul). The soul must discard the body so it can turn to dust, and the soul can go home. This is a pure white light, a clean, bright, and beautiful act that brings a bright essence to each and every soul. This is the eternal one, not the body. The body is not eternal and has an expiration date in this dimension of time and space. It must fall off as it gets used up like any useful thing. The little soul leaves it and goes into its eternal home, to wait for the rest of the little souls, constantly arriving to greet it.

What is inside the home? Me, God, my angels, and thousands, millions, billions of souls, my fairies, and other beings of the elements. We are all there as one big family, you are coming after us. This is our kingdom, and you will love it.

Your GOD.

"The light conditions the loudness of your heart and love you have for yourself."

13th message: HAPPINESS IS SOMETHING WONDERFUL

Dear Sandra,

My angel, I'm connecting with you so you can take the following message to the world. You, my angel, shall spread my message to the people of the world, as you are my emissary tasked to tell it. What shall we talk about today? Today, we will share something about **happiness**.

What is happiness? Happiness is something so wonderful it defies description. It must be felt; it must be carried inside oneself as a mother carries her child for 9 months. Happiness is the authenticity present when chills envelop your entire body when you smell the most beautiful flowers, which in your blessed state seem like diamonds, and when you cannot do anything else but fly as angels fly on their wings. But what hides beneath this feeling, this feeling of happiness? A bit of positive vibration, positive energy running through your veins, chakras, and body, and returns downwardly around the body. It circles here and there around the body and tingles our nostrils, so it sometimes just hurts. We are glued to this feeling, all proud and beautiful. Our body shines with health, our hair is vibrant, our smile and will are august. What fathers this beautiful feeling? Something magnificent, even the metaphysics cannot describe.

Can you imagine a big round glass ball? Within it is only light and nothing else. Looking inside, you see nothing in the ball. There is nothing inside, except a special kind of light, something within it that attracts our gaze, and we look inside. We look and look and see nothing. Then the sun shines, our feeling of happiness, and the ball then brightly shines. It is then that we see it, no longer an empty glass shell, but a shining, at times golden, beautiful ball that awakens within us beautiful feelings, feelings at the highest vibration, the vibration of happiness…

That's it. Once you feel it, you know it. What brings the feeling of happiness that, like the wax of bees in a hive, flows through our veins? All the good, everything that makes us happy. A new car, a newborn child, or maybe a new bag? No. The little things, even the littlest things, that make us grateful, because we have them, see them, feel them, and give them. When we are grateful, we are happy. When we are happy, we experience it as a feeling of profound happiness. But when we are not happy, we of course can't be happy. We don't have that feeling then. When we see a small white butterfly flying from flower to flower, it is a scene of a happy person seeing and feeling the beauty of nature. This small piece of the feeling of happiness can be felt every day, every minute, and every moment. Catch it, my dear friends, as it is precious. Do not count money, do not just watch the beauty in expensive things and brands, as these will not bring you these feelings of happiness. Your happiness is born within you. First, inside yourself, there is where you must find happiness first, within yourself. To make others happy and to see others happy, you must be happy with yourself. But these things will not be the ones that bring happiness, as you are already happy.

Can you *gift* your happiness? You can. With a smile, a shake of a hand, with spirituality, with something beautiful that someone else will cherish and will brighten their day. But even they will already have to be happy with themselves if they wish to feel the gifted piece of happiness.

Happiness does not roll outside your door, your eyes, or your threshold. You have it in your hands. Hold it tight so it does not slip through your fingers.

Your God.

"Happiness is on the side of those who know what hides within them."

14th message: TIME DOES NOT EXIST, SPACE IS NOT SEEN ...

Dear Sandra,

My angel, today I will talk about **time**. Write down my message for the people of the world.

The clarity of life begins when we start to feel our souls, when we are willing to give ourselves to others, and give up just enjoying material things. That is true life, as our time, the time that chases us, is too short to live a life where we do bad things, craft delusions, and wait to die. Waiting by the watch does not bring good results. These eternal indicators of our time insist we work by a temporal system that is preaching endlessly, pointing to a time that is nothing but an illusion. Why would we only be in this time frame, which not only belongs to us now while living it, but also in other dimensions?

Have you ever asked yourself what drives you through the day? Your clock that ticks and tocks on your arm, your nightstand, your wall, and tells you, you must do things within a certain time frame. No, you do not have to because this is all an illusion. That is not the way to think about the life you're living. Go and see something that will drive you away from the creation of time. Give it time, the saying goes. And what does it say? You must always wait for some time to pass. But why wait and restrict yourself to two hands on a watch, which doesn't mean anything? It doesn't mean the time or purpose you must fulfill at the required time. The best of music is written in a timeless space. Time does not exist.

Space also does not exist. Space is measured by people. This great big chest, that stalks you and tick-tocks in the greatest possible time machine, is slowly moving away from human life and going to another level. A level unseen and unknown to you. Don't you know that I, God, am timeless, invisible, and can go anywhere at any time?

And what of you people? You are limited by a component of time, which you call time. The hands on your expensive watches are timeless and incomplete in the sense that you do not need them, and they are not useful.

Who are the hands on the watch supposed to be useful for? What do you get from limiting yourself to a single dimension of time, when you can be everywhere else? Can you imagine being on your couch and also being at a football game? No. Because you are limited by a time component, you call it time. You respect it so much you die on time, mate on time, go on diets according to the moon, cut your hair on time, garden and plant on time, remove the weeds on time... But what does it bring you? Something intangible that is only limiting you. Know that this does not exist on God's estate. Does not exist. I can, like you, be everywhere. At the ice cream shop, barber, bakery, school, on a bus, grabbing a coffee... And you? You cannot be in the same place at the same time, as you are also limited by space.

See all the limitations that you have. Time and space. Do you think it is right that you can go from point A to B only when the train is there to take you? To listen to music that is only on at certain times on certain stations? I can do anything, anywhere.

The purpose of life is not to limit, but my dear friends is a beautiful melodic music that accompanies us from birth till death and is accompanied by all the Godly ingredients the universe, I, God, provides. Take them if you want. You must only want it.

Only that. Is it the gravest sin if a person does not wish to get up at a certain early hour? Time does not exist; space cannot be seen. They are illusions. So be patient and get used to the order out of time and space in which we are all one, timeless, and filled with love.

Your God.

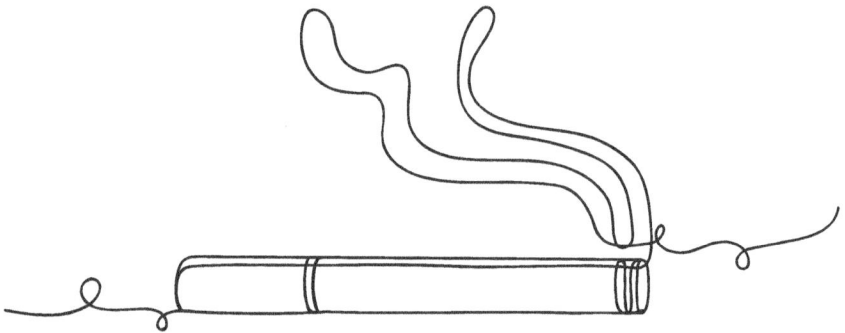

"Do not carry around weapons if you don't know how to shoot.
You can hurt yourself and others. Instead, spread love with a smile,
feeling of happiness, longing, joy, and life in white."

15th message: CONSCIOUS ADDICTION

Divinity is within you, my dear angel Sandra. Today, we will give the world a message about **conscious addiction**, which baffles people and pushes them into addiction to a great many things. People are addicted to drugs, relationships, medication, and substances, and this must stop.

On a collective level, this is just too much. Every day, I watch people taking every type of drug, intoxicating themselves, and getting drunk. This is not good for the mind, body, or soul. These substances are the source of all evil, which, for a moment, push the body and soul into ecstasy, so it bears fruit to new conquering plans that lead to unhealthy patterns. People, you must also stop your addiction to relationships! You are addicted to the relationships with your daughters, mothers, brothers, sisters, and partners that bind you to them. Here is the key to removing these disorders: just love. It heals all disorders. You cannot live on substances and situations of dependence, which push every single person into a destructive relationship, filled with only trauma and incorrect decisions. Go and free yourself of these chains. May the shadow of your medication, cocaine, and dependency fall into the water, whose current will take it away.

Pictures of destitute addicts force themselves into my eyes every time I see them, when with one shot, one dose, they try to save themselves before a flood of unwise choices and selfish threats to their mind and body. Do you think that your actions with the needle, which only bring you to the current ecstasy of intoxication, are going to bring you into a better tomorrow? Never. Your brain, an intoxicated brain, does not work right. You are not led by the hand of God in these moments; you are led by your ego, which again received a dose of self-respect. Confirmation of his victory. The ego.

That devil's symbol inside of you that lurks and waits to outfox you and say: "Come, give me another dose, it'll make you feel better, you will work better, and you will love all around you but yourself the most." Don't listen to him! Don't listen to the ego, the enemy of the soul, who calls and calls and leads you into the greatest depths of your despair, idleness, and homelessness, and away from the love for yourself and others. The Earth needs those who will work with love, not ego.

What are the relationships of dependence? The most widely spread and biggest menace in this society. They menace every corner, every step, when your ego takes you by your hand and brings you into a relationship of dependence with your partner, spouse, or child, your mother, father, son, coffee, tea, and anything else…

What will you do to turn away from destructive relationships that push you to addiction? When you do not exist by yourself without the hand of someone else to guide you. When you cannot exist by yourself without having the hand of someone else to guide you, when you can't sleep, eat, or pee without someone to whom you're addicted? Because your happiness is only dependent on that exact ego-drenched living being and your relationship with them.

Let go of these bands of addiction, which are making you sick. Do you really think you cannot be happy by yourself? Why? Because you do not love yourself, that is why you cannot be happy. First, feel the love towards yourself. It will not lead you into a relationship of addiction filled with unloving fights or addictive hand-holding with your partner. People, it must take you to the skies, where you will become independent of it all, except yourself! You will only be addicted to yourself!

Do you know how it is to be only dependent on yourself? To see inside yourself and love yourself and feel the happiness and harmony inside your body, you love. That is how you can spread and receive your happiness. It is then that you are not led by the hand of ego, that is when your ego sleeps and isn't there. Then you know that you are in tune with yourself and that the ego is not present, is not there. That is when you love yourself so much that you wish to share the happiness. That is when you do not need an addiction, as your heart is lively, happy, and content.

Running from yourself in addictive relationships is like running from a bull that wants to gore you with its horns. Don't run, the light is already inside you. Just turn it on, let it shine, and light up the world. Be happy, friend, it is the greatest medicine you can give yourself or others. Not a medicine that numbs you like some dastardly chemical, not a relationship that drags you into an even greater pit of addiction, you alone, my friend, are your own best medicine. Not pharmaceuticals. Not cocaine. Not drugs. You.

Find this medicine within yourself and heal yourself each day. Drink it like you're swallowing a pill, a drug, an addictive relationship, or motherhood, because then your heart will be completely healthy and your mind positive, happy, relaxed, and it will take you to a soul that sings. When you become your own best friend, you will not need the hand of another, will not need ego to wake you up, will not need the neighbor, mother, or child to make you happy, just yourself. Your heart will beat from the perfect love like a full cup of all non-addictive substances. Drink it and heal yourself.

Your God.

"There is nothing more beautiful than to be loved.
To love and be loved. This is priceless and cannot be bought,
only lived. Simply lived. "

16th message: LOVE IS THE GREATEST TREASURE

What is written is my message. From God. Today, you, my angel Sandra, carry my message. Come, let's talk about the greatest treasure a person can possess. **LOVE**. This is a book about love, right? This is a book about love, pure love, that will heal each and every person who reads it. Why?

Because it is written with my love, the divine light I passed down through her hand, aura, and through her pen. I wish that love, my dear friends, reaches all of you, all the billions that live in this world. It will bring you healing! Sandra is writing a book that will heal you! Remember every letter written down, as they will heal. My light through her pen spreads through the words you're reading. What are you reading? About love? Yes, about love. Love is the ruler of the world. It should be, although it's not always. That is why I sprinkle it and give it out through her pen into the words you're reading or are going to read.

This is a book about love.

It heals. How? Why? In what way can it heal us, you say? Like this: "Read every letter, first L, then O, then V, then E. All of them… You can read them together or apart – all from the word **'love'**."

What do my dear friends, do you feel, when they read each letter apart or all of them together? What does it feel like when you first just see and then also read?

What do you see? A whiteness, white radiance, shine, gold, silver, something beautiful? Or something black, blue, dark, or maybe fear? Well, what? What do you see and feel at the word "love", the letters that comprise it? What are your feelings? Is it beautiful and good? Is it relaxing, calming, makes you swoon, and warms your heart? It does, doesn't it? It is a good word, it is not black, but white. It is love. Write it down somewhere and feel it twenty times, a million times a day if you want; and with it feel all the things that word expresses. What will you squeeze into the word "love"? Think and feel what goes inside. Do this twenty times a day, and it will heal you! My dear friends, just by reading it and feeling it, you will – believe me – be cured.

Can you feel it healing you a little?
This whiteness, which is carried by the word "l o v e".

This is your daily mantra; learn to use it every day and every hour.

How can letters heal you, you may ask? Well, they can. In every message Sandra writes for you, I'm bringing healing energy, filled with love. Every single time she writes at her white desk, her white dress, her white-lacquered nails, sitting next to white candles in front of a radiant silver healing heart on a white altar. She is conductive, a conduit for the light, the symbol of health and healing, which I'm passing down to you from the sphere of the divine into this book. Read love, and you will be healed when reading those lines. This is your medicine; you need nothing else. Read these lines, absorb them, and every day open your chakra of love into which you will, with your feelings and thought patterns through reading this book, bring in light, white, and love. This is how your heart will become even more receptive to the giving and receiving of love. Receive it in these lines.

Your God.

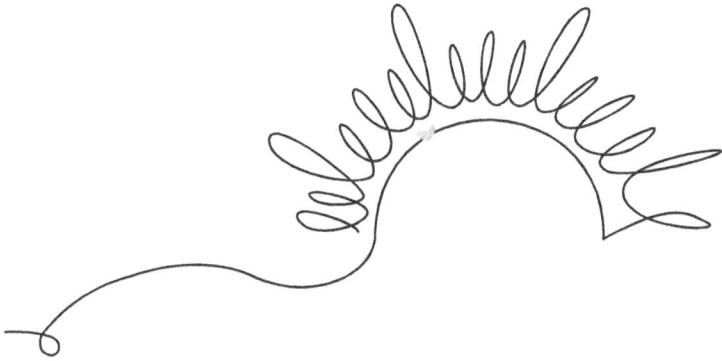

"Look at the walls of your room.
They reflect your breath upon them."

14th September 2019

17th message: DIVINE LOVE IS ALWAYS WITHIN US

Dear Sandra,

My angel, today we will write about **"the love from beyond"**. Love that comes from me, the divine world, the sphere of God, is pure, beautiful, and is within you every day, my friends. Located deep inside, you must only look to find it. It is the purest energy of the universe, the energy of all creation. It is love, pure love, that shields your bodies and endows them with a pure layer of love that never fades. Take it, drink from it as a cup, for then you are a divine being of pure love.

I, God, am in you every minute of every day. We are not separate people; I am inside you, always. You cannot be separate from me, because when you are, it is no longer you. After all, you are no longer the pure true love. I see many people separated from the universal love of God, their hearts not beating with the rhythm of love it does when they are with me. That is when their mind - their ego - is talking, which makes them miserable in all areas of their life. Friends, why do you separate from me when I am your fountain of life? This separation from me, the authenticity, which every moment leads you down the right path, is not a joke. Do not think of bad things, do not separate your ignorant ego, stained with dirty thoughts, from your divinity. The divinity that does not sleep and lies within you is the most beautiful blossom and the most beautiful flower in the meadow. Do you know what a wilted flower looks like? Nothing pretty to look at – wrinkled, poor, disheveled! When you separate from the divine energy and love, you become like that flower. No longer living, but dying.

Not alive. Do you know what the old people used to say? If it's not worth looking at, it's not worth eating. Your life on earth then means nothing. You are just traveling through galaxies that are not your own, get lost in them, and do things that do not become you.

Find the divine in limitless quantities within yourself. No one will take it away, no one will steal it. You create, possess, and have it yourself. Why do you think you need to give it to someone? Everyone has it within themselves, they must but use it. Are you living it? No! When I look at people, most are not connected to me and are separating themselves from me. This is not good. Why are you doing this? Come, connect with yourself, go into nature, write, draw, paint, do the things you love, kiss each other, live your dream because dreams are real, and do things with a sense of happiness and satisfaction. When you do you are connected to yourself and you love to live, you are connected to me, God. It is then that you are living like you should. Do you feel my limitless love, which I give you now and always?

You have to! Because I am the one who gives you life, breath, beauty, creativity, life in spirit, and not this wretched life many people live. You did not come down here to cry, live in misery, shoot each other, die young, and live unreal lives devoid of love. You came to enjoy, love, create, spread, have a wonderful time, caress each other, and explore. What of life if you do not feel that my friends?

What good will all the money of this world do when you do not have it and constantly live in misery? But it is here, it is always here. Everything is already here. Everything is in your palm, everything is in abundance, and everything in this divine universe is in abundance for everyone! For each person! Do you hear me? Pick it up, take what you want, nothing is limited; it is all in your head. It angers me to see people who could have it all, love, happiness, money, great relationships, beautiful loving partnerships, but they are always without these things as they simply do not take them. Take it, my dear friends, it is here all the time, right beside you, just take it, like going out to gather the flowers or getting food at the market!

Thinking things are limited and in short supply is limiting. They are not! You only think this way. After all, you are limited in mind, because you are not soaked with divine energy given to you freely and limitlessly from me, and you are SEPARATE from me!

Remember one thing – we are all ONE! I am within you every second, every moment, every day, just do not try to separate from me. Divine love is constantly wrapped around you, but do not try to rip it off or out of yourself. Let it be, let it guard and lead you, and let it be your guide and lover throughout your life as a manifested being on earth.

The Earth is round, right? You know this! But how do you know it's round? Have you seen it with your own eyes? No, you saw it in pictures. They told you! Well, now listen and understand and believe me when I say that your divinity, my love, light, and radiance have been within you from the first moment you were born and cried into the world. But somewhere along the way, my friends, you separated yourselves from it! Now you must make sure that my light, radiance, and love are always present within you because they are (you rip these out and separate yourselves). And remember, we are all **ONE**!

Your God.

"A horse you cannot saddle is hard to ride.
Prepare it for the finest race. Let this be the race of your life where
every time you take the lead, you slow down. "

18th message: THE MAGICAL DAY AND THE WHEEL OF HAPPINESS

Dear Sandra,

My angel, I am here and I'm connecting with you. Your energy is now directed into your pen. Do you see the light which is always here? The light of divinity is all around us, and our beings are beings of light if we allow them. You do not need rituals if your whiteness and light are not present.

This is what I have to say. What kind of day is a magical day when you see the light that intertwines in your thoughts? Have you ever created a magical day in your life? The magic that is your thoughts, actions, and all you do, the pure love you give yourself and the world. When your heart is open to a million beautiful things that give you harmony, balance, and even greater love in life. You know, every day can be magical. Do you know that you can make it so that it is devoid of your personal fears, devoid of your dancing on a thin sheet of fear, and drenched in clean, pure love? Do you then also know that you can be in the greatest state of allowing? That you can receive absolutely anything when you are in the blessed state, the state of light, on that magical day? When you dance and do not run into a wall, when there are no obstacles to lead you to unthinking acts, no feelings of fear, dancing on the hard floor of fear and apprehension, but is only love.

Come, make each day a magical day, so your thoughts will be your own magnificent creations, which will only go into the beautiful kingdoms of your soul. These will be wonderful days threaded through with happiness and contentment that will, through these feelings, heal your soul bit by bit. Are you ever led by a feeling that you would just like to dance and love yourself to bits? That is the true feeling, the feeling of happiness that keeps you in harmony and compatible with your inner divine. Don't fight it, just give in. Do not work from the mind, work from the soul. The soul knows what it wants. Listen to it! Do you know what your soul is? It is your body, but not your physical body with your bones, cells, sinew, heart, hair, and skin, but your real body, which you must feed with real food to keep it happy and content. Only a happy soul lives. It is not dead. This happy soul takes you into the channel world of beauty, the world through which you manifest into your fleshy body. Let it breathe and sing, because that is when it's happy, beautiful, and filled with divine grace.

And happy is your day when you create an event that makes your soul sing. It should sing every day because that is when it is at home in the white, beautiful world that is paradise to her. Create your own wonderful day, for this, you require nothing and no one. Beautiful things, beautiful relationships, a wonderful mind, these things are created by you, my friends. Do not rely on anyone, on anything.

Nobody will make you happy, and nothing will give you personal happiness. This happiness must come from within; it lies inside of you as it already is inside of you, so do not search for happiness outside of yourself. When you do I, God is not inside you. That is when you are separated from me. Do you understand that everything is already inside of you? Nothing you seek is outside of you. You're searching in vain. You are responsible for your own happiness, your own wonderful day, and your entire life.

Is it hard to overcome yourself and venture forth into each new, wonderful day? It's not! Every day can be perfectly wonderful if you want it to be. If you wish it to be, then make it so. Yes, make it beautiful, what are you waiting for? Do not wait for people to make you happy, because that is not what you see. Have you met a favorite animal? You have? Then keep it, so you can love it and bring it forth from within yourself, but you can only do that if you find your source, the well of happiness within. The animal will only be useful with decisions around the vibrational well of happiness, which will grow and raise the surface of the water in your balanced body and mind. But do not punish yourself with misery, which never brings you and your loved ones anything good, because misery spreads, and your relationships will be miserable.

Why do people constantly cry about their unhappiness? Because they're not. Their slice of perspective that they can see and hold on to only leads to a cursed infinity and cursed colors. They continue drawing with these colors that are outside the divine harmony. The canvas is always there, it just has to be painted following the divine, does it not?

I am telling you, your God, that you are divine and that your calling has already been determined outside the range of your senses, which sometimes tell you differently and lead you to a different path. Why walk down a different, unpaved road when you can walk down a safe, clean, paved, beautiful road? Are you aware of your actions concerning this planet, all its people, and its living beings when you for yourself and others pave these beautiful roads? This way is leading you to a better tomorrow for everyone on this little Earth. So continue creating these straight, beautiful, and well-traveled roads for you, your loved ones, and all the people in the world.

Is it necessary to always take the difficult path to get to the top and tackle difficult uphill situations in the hardest way possible? No. You already have everything, my friends, right in your own hands. Just use them, but allow yourself to use them most authentically and perfectly. What drives you to be unhappy, filled with dislike, constant antipathy, and unkindness to your fellow beings?

This will not benefit you; that is not love. I'm telling you to just love yourself, first love yourself, and then everybody else, because it is only in that way that the world will shine in the bright and white light of the world. There will be no smoke, no layer of fear, insecurity, ugly things, merely a white planet with beautiful people, whose every day of the year is magical.

If you can find magic every day, then you are loved, filled with wonderful ideas and beautiful acts that brighten up your fellow human's day. Do you think your dog does not feel when you are happy, and you give him back even more love than he gives you? Of course, he does. Then give love. To the dog, the fish, the donkey, the beautiful cow, the zebra, the most beautiful butterfly, the earth, your mother, the most beautiful child, and all creation. Inspire the earth with beautiful acts and beautiful situations, which will make it even more beautiful and marvelous, all 365 days of the year that you humans count. You have nothing to lose, right? Except for the fact that you're unhappy and apathetic, you have nothing to lose.

But what drives you to be apathetic, hateful, and rigid in your behavior? Because you manifest out of yourself, and you do not love yourself! Friend, look in the mirror, love yourself. Tell yourself two hundred times a day that you are beautiful, polite, compassionate, and that you are **infinitely fond of yourself** -- that you love yourself. That, my friend, is the love for yourself. To your head and your feelings. The energy of love changes everything. And when you vibrate on the frequency of love, turn away from the mirror and take this love you have for yourself and spread it out into the world. It will open every door, everywhere, in your beautiful relationships, in the behavior of others towards yourself, in beautiful things that you will invite into your magical day, in beautiful situations which will take you even higher to a greater love, where you will fly on the wings of love like a bird. You do wish to be a bird on the wings of love, right?

That is when you feel me, God, in all the beauty and divinity that flows from the ball of beauty inside your body, your aura, into every being on this planet. Is it not wonderful when someone smiles at you? Are your feelings better than are you relaxed? Of course, you are. Because everything is energy. The energy that raises your vibration to a higher level and makes you even happier, you can pass this love onto others with a simple smile. But you have to create the conditions so you can smile first. So you can be the one smiling and give this smile to others. It is like a boomerang that comes back to you. What you give out, you will receive back. What am I trying to tell you about this magical day? Let your happiness sprout within you, grow, and shine outward. You will feel it, and that will make you even happier as you make others happy, and they bring the happiness back to you. This is **the wheel of happiness**.

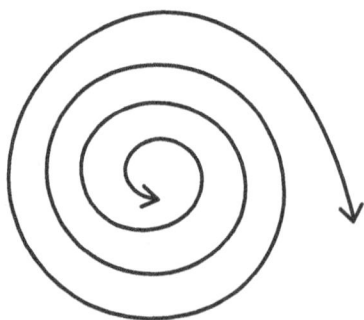

WHEEL OF HAPPINESS AND LOVE

You see, the wheel of happiness spins in both directions! You give and receive. The other receives what he gives. It is so simple. You must only allow yourself to feel the glory and feel only love. That is the one and only rule.

Feel love.

Live love.

Give in to love.

Bring love to the world.

Grow the most beautiful thoughts.

Be a person in all his glory.

Observe the light which always shines for you,

even in your darkest moments!

Be who you are!

Be light, be divinity!

Your God.

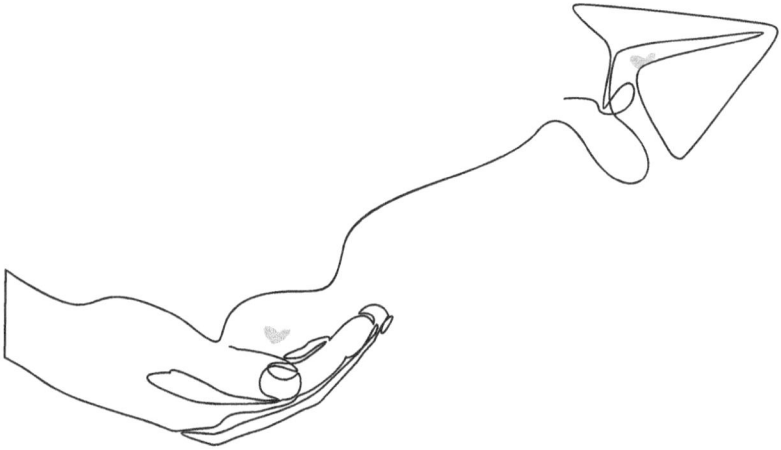

"There are no souls more worthy than us. There are only souls that live here or in the other world."

19th message: GET RID OF HATE. HATE IS NOT GOD'S WORK

Dear Sandra,

My angel, today we are going to be writing about hate again. It is an evil in this world, so I wish to tell people to get rid of it. Live without this tireless devil, which sometimes and maybe even all the time watches over them and pushes them into a timeless hell. This emotion is divisive because it is not an emotion that bears any resemblance to God's love. Not everyone is capable of it, but I see that people occasionally and sometimes even constantly harbor hateful thoughts and perform hateful acts that they cannot face, and in so doing kill every piece of their God-given heart.

Hatred is an emotion that people most of the time harbor as a grudge against someone they wish to get revenge against. Hatred is an emotion that people don't like. However, their ego inexplicably kills and thrums their heartstrings, which are now intertwined like a net cast in the shadow of the greatest light and are unable to help them anymore. Then fear starts to inhabit their hearts, which dooms them, squeezes them, drains their energy, and drains them.

This fear is terribly stressful for the human body. It must be immediately shaken off because it is not illumination, not the light. It is the energy that kills, which does not enrich a person but makes him weaker and keeps him eternally poor. They cannot escape the clutches that doom them, so this person must enter a meditative state or yoga, where they can calm down, find their wounded heart, and soothe the hurt.

May hatred disappear from the minds of men, because this emotion does no good for anyone. Nobody deserves it. Nobody deserves to hate, and nobody deserves to be hated. That is not God's work. It is the work of the "small" people, who wish to use their power in an unloving way, a way not given by God.

So, what to do when you feel the hate inside of yourself? Find the healing energies of nature that are waiting for you in the forest, in the shape of the trees, plants, sun, and clean air, because that is where you'll find me, God, in all my glory and beauty. You will meet me there.

Sit next to the creek, sit next to the water that you see, and close your eyes. Your eyes in these moments feel as if they weigh a million tons, as you don't see right and don't see a lot. That is when you see evil, the evil that does not belong to you and does not fit you. Sit, raise your hands, and connect with me. Connect with God, connect with the illumination, connect with the light. Be a child again, be a small child who has just been born. Be alone with yourself. Ask all the angels and me, God, to clear your heart of all the ungodly and hateful thoughts, so that it becomes shining, white, and pure.

Then, in the purest beauty and grace, only feel the love. And spell the word "love". Feel it in your heart. Let it flare up in your entire body from head to toe. Send all your fears and ugly thoughts to us in the light. Be and become the light that shines in this kingdom of people and beings, yourself for a time. Sit there and enjoy the harmony and give yourself over to the hands of God.

Your heart will sing. Do this meditation seven times a week in nature, and you will see the emotion of hate disappear. Look at people with eyes of beauty. Your heart will become softer, and the stories you will be able to tell will be beautiful and not filled with hate.

Dear human, first stop hating yourself. Stop it, you hear! You need to stop this like a jockey stops his steed. STOP! Can you hear me? That is the first step that you must take. Stop hating yourself. Hatred of self is the worst and lowest emotion, which will lead you to your doom. Think to yourself that you are a being with the most beautiful body, and begin to love absolutely everything about yourself. Let your day start with love for yourself and the abandonment of every inkling of that vicious emotion of hate. Hatred for yourself and consequently others leads you to disease. You feel the cells of your body decay and start to rot; when you hate yourself, you are also hating every other person and are sending the energy of hate into the world. The energy of hate that is destroying the world.

Do you know what a beautiful world this would be if the whole world only sent the energy of love out to this little beautiful blue marble? It would be paradise. Paradise for all the people who love themselves and love others. But why then would you rather pick hatred than love for yourself and others? There is a reason this is inside you. Because you feel guilty because you do not love yourself 100 percent, because you are not beautiful, because you have been imprinted with old patterns, and are hateful towards yourself. But the knowledge you have about yourself – the knowledge of hate - erases it from your mind. The head becomes lighter, clearer, and they think effortlessly without the constant hateful thoughts about themselves, their being, their heart, and their beautiful body.

You are a Godly being, and if you are Godly, you cannot and should not ever harbor hateful suicidal thoughts towards yourself. Yes, you read that right, hateful thoughts are suicidal because they are killing you every second, every moment, and you cannot operate like that. So, you must stop it. Begin to look at yourself in the mirror in the morning, look into your lovely eyes, and say:

"You are love, you are a divine being, you are radiance, you are love, you are light. I like myself, I love myself, I am eternal, I am indispensable to the faults of others, I am not separate from God, we are all one. I love all living creatures, I love people.
I LOVE MYSELF."

Repeat this every day, every morning, 10 minutes in front of a mirror, look into your eyes and feel the light infuse your body and heart, and be clean. Your eyes will see a different image in the mirror, your eyes will become loving, and your body will become pure love. Spread this love and give it to the world.

Your God.

"It is wise to fly with one's wings rather than those of another. Those will not take you far. "

By the river Ižica, 16th September 2019

20th message: BE THE BRIGHTEST AND MOST BEAUTIFUL LIGHTBULB – LIGHT OF THE WORLD

Dear Sandra,

My angel incarnate, what do I have to tell you today? A lot. A great many things that people must hear as soon as possible. You act as my extended hand as you write the words I'm about to say.

Write it down:

1. Friends, love yourself each day! Each day, tell yourself how immensely you love yourself, respect yourself, and value yourself. Your energy is something to behold when it is white and shines outwards into the dark.

2. Give yourself only the best. Go into nature and surround yourself with angelic energy, and the elvish beauty of plants, and do not lust for shopping malls, consumerism, and shopping. Leave your addictions, the drugs that drag you down into idleness and empty out your soul, behind! Go to the coffee shop and order the biggest ice cream if you want it. Why not? Let it be healthy, and your desire for it should be quenched if you wish it, and God gifts it. God gives everything, just make sure that you enjoy the ice cream endlessly! Enjoy! That is the condition when you give yourself that scoop of sweetness. If it is still healthy, then you are also healed and served.

3.	Be calm. Calm your mind, think beautiful, happy, loving, pure thoughts of love. Do you still remember how to spell "love"? What do you feel? You feel something beautiful! And again, you enjoy, immeasurably, hearing this marvelous word. When gripped by fear and negative thoughts, immediately turn and remember this word. Sing it, sing this word! Write it down and feel good, enjoy the word! If unhappy thoughts overtake you, sing this word as loudly as you can! So loud that the whole world can hear! Sing it in the tones of the songs you love the most.

4.	Love all the people! Love all the people around you, and with this love, heal them as well as yourself. When you love, respect, and cherish them, it means you also love yourself. Can you imagine what a wonder drug this tablet is when you love yourself and others? How does this "love for others" have a healing effect on them and yourself? It heals like all the Ibuprofens of this world. Your "love for others" also heals the earth and allows it to be born in this beautiful love. Can you imagine if all day, every day, everyone would love themselves and others? Oh, this world, this planet, would be beautiful. Bathed in pure love.

5.	Why trouble yourself with worry when you do not have to? What are you worried about? What is "worry"? The fear, illusion, just your fear that never leads you anywhere. Drop your worries when they grab onto you, throw them, pack them up in a balloon, a white balloon, pick up the balloon, close your eyes, and throw it away, far away, throw it into space, into the white light and then spell, "l o v e". Stop at the letter L. What is it trying to tell you? Love, *liebe*, *ljubezen*, lovely, longing, living… think of all of these. What else do you think about when you, my dears, see and **feel** the letter L. Connect it to something beautiful. With love. With this, everything will improve, and you will see your worries disappear. If just the L is not enough, then move to the letter O, and so on. You will see, your worries will fly away, and you will be reborn.

6. Why walk the path that is not yours? The path isn't yours when you're not yourself and are separated from God, the radiant divine light. When separated, you are not yourself, my friends. You walk the path that is not yours. Leave that path, turn around, and walk your path on which you don't look back, you just are, and you look, and you walk and do nothing where you're going and why you're going... you are here and now. Here you are with God. Here you are ONE with God and the divine energy within, while on this path, when you just walk and are here and now.

7. Why would your thoughts contain unhealthy air breathed in every day, over negative messages, news, people, media across the world, and all the negative things that surround you? Leave that behind and go into nature, seize nature, and relax far away from mobile phones, TV screens, beaming lamps, artificial lights, and dependent earthly things... Go, feed your soul in nature – with the sound of the birds, bubbling streams, rustling grasses, and smells of aromatic great big trees. Go and love yourself and love nature, you can see the surroundings around you. Don't sit caged inside four walls, don't travel all the time with vehicles, don't talk on your phones, and don't sit in coffee shops and shopping centers. Go outside into NATURE. Nature will allow you

to once again re-establish the link between yourself, your divinity, and me, God.

8.   Think about being ONE with every human being, one with nature, all the animals, Muslims, Catholics, and Jews, with every single solitary person of any denomination. Understand that you are one with **everyone** and **everything**. You are ONE because you are the spark of divine light that smolders and rests in you and every living and nonliving being, in everything, within EVERYTHING.

The human race is immensely loving until it steps out of its divinity, until people stop loving themselves and those around them. A human born in all his splendor did not arrive here to suffer. He is beautiful and immensely loving in his soul until separated from his true self, his true essence. In this state, he will do things that do not come from himself but from his ego. Then his separation does not come from him and his essence, but from his inner lower self.

But what is the lower self? It is not a small, tiny creature called a dwarf, but the body and the mind of a human. When he starts to think and do things based on his body and mind, we call that his lower self or ego.

The ego is the little worm, the little tiny worm in your mind that attacks us every time we are separated from our higher inner self, our light, our grace, our beauty, our beautiful actions, and our devout universal spiritual thoughts. When separated, we are filled with nothing beautiful; we become like ugly elves or dragons, and we take it out on ourselves and others. Why, for God's sake? We don't have to do this. We don't have to allow the ego to attack; you do not have to be separated from the light, from your higher self.

THE HIGER SELF =
your soul, your light, that
radiates your "love"

This is your primordial self, it is you – the light of the world – born from divine energy, from divine light. As the most beautiful, brightest radiating bulb. Do you know the intricacies of the light you give off? They are divine. Connected with God, with yourself, with your beauty and pure love.

Your God.

"It's smarter to do big things than bother with small unworthy things that only look big. These do not make a person beautiful, but different. The God of the unknown."

By the river Ižica, 17th September 2019

21st message: JOY, THE MILLIONAIRE GAME, AND THE HELIUM BALLOON

Dear Sandra,

My angel, you are my extension, my hand that serves the people and is their medicine. What I tell you now is very important.

Let the spark of joy shine in your eyes as you write this.

Today, dear friends, let me tell you the story of eternal joy on this planet. It is the guarantee of happiness in your life. JOY. The joy you decide to have in your life, the joy you write about, and the joy you live. You must be joyous every day. You must choose it. You are the smith of your fortune, as a blacksmith forging the shoes for the horse. Will he make a beautifully designed horseshoe, or will he decide to make an ugly one? How do you decide when you get out of bed in the morning? Do you stretch, yawn, and say: "Oh, what a beautiful day it is today, I'm going to enjoy this!" or do you say "Ugh, what an awful day, another boring day of misery and trauma! The boss will yell at me again, the wife and kids will be annoying, I'll miss the flight, the food is gonna suck." Will you choose joy, my friend? Will you choose to meet with joy, happiness, and gladness, and open up your beautiful divine eyes wide, open up your arms wide towards the heavens, and wish yourself a beautiful day? Or will you sigh and decide to live your day in the same chaos as yesterday? What will you decide?

You know, this is the **decision**. The big one. A decision that will imprint your vibration for the entire day and leave a mark on not just your own daily life, but also your surroundings and the entire planet. What do I mean by the entire planet? How are you, small, tiny, insignificant, helpless little things that call yourself people supposed to affect the whole planet with the joy you can decide on in the morning? It's not possible you'll cry out.

But it is! It is! Listen well! You will do what you choose in the morning. If you open your wallet in the morning and see you only have a dollar and then complain how you don't have any money and are living a life of deprivation (my dear friends, these are the thoughts of deprivation and not the abundance you are meant to have to live well), you will be like that your entire day. You will play the game and the day of the poor man. The poor man is still losing his money. His pockets will be empty all day, and bills will keep piling up, as you have to pay for this and that… a bottomless pit. Your vibration will be low. Because you saw poverty in that one dollar, you will play the poor man's play all day, and you will cry and moan instead of playing the millionaire game. Play the second game! You must only decide, my dear friends.

Drink tea in the morning, and before heading out, look at that one dollar (although you are right, it is just a dollar) and **play the millionaire game**. Make the choice that you are very wealthy with one dollar. Feel as if you are incredibly wealthy. Just think of all the things you could buy with that one dollar. How many things in fact! Put it in your wallet, go to the store, and you will see that for a single dollar, you can buy a thousand things. Feel this fortune, feel how for a single dollar you can afford a hundred, a thousand things. That is when you'll bring the feeling of a rich man. It does not matter if you're only holding a dollar, I'm telling you that you should rather feel, truly feel, just shaking at the thought of all you can buy for such a sum! You can feel it, can't you?

1 $	100 things	100 $
	1.000 things	1.000 $
	1.000.000 things	1.000.000 $

Do you see these numbers, how you can have a hundred dollars, a thousand dollars, a million dollars? Neat, isn't it? Yes, you truly can be rich, my dear friends, if you only **allow** it and **decide** it! You can do the same as the example everywhere. Just have JOY as your companion as you joyfully enter a new day and think like this – and not just about money, but about everything, about love, relationships, good things…When you are joyful, the joy brings you even more joy and more abundance. Life is meant to be enjoyed and to be **lived** and not meant for dying.

Remember this and write it down:

"Life is to be lived. Life is not for dying.
Life is not dying in poverty, in not having, in misfortunes,
sadness, and fear!"

How will you **live**, my friends? Like I've just told you. The smallest joyous thought that, like a balloon, blows up into a thousand other joyous thoughts (you know thoughts breed like rabbits). If you raise one thought, it breeds another, and that one a third and fourth and so on… Thousands, millions of good, beautiful thoughts about plenty, beauty, relationships, love, nonattachment, joy, and happiness.

This is the process I call the **Helium balloon**. A thought is like a helium balloon. If you start with one nice thought, it will multiply and expand over the day multiply and expand like the helium that fills up a balloon.

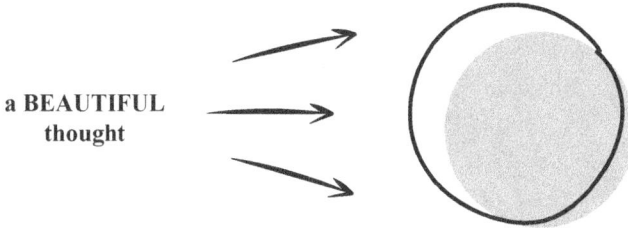

a BEAUTIFUL
thought

My dear friends, if every person filled each day with thousands, millions of such helium balloons, what would this world, this planet, be like? Immensely beautiful.

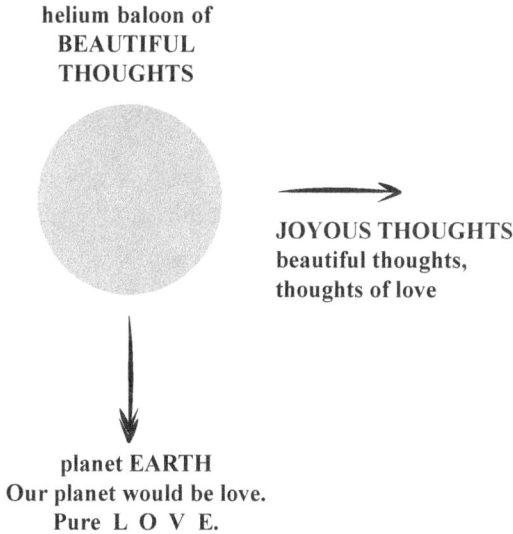

helium baloon of
**BEAUTIFUL
THOUGHTS**

JOYOUS THOUGHTS
beautiful thoughts,
thoughts of love

planet EARTH
Our planet would be love.
Pure L O V E.

But it's not. Why? Because people do not think only good thoughts. They have fears, insecurities, and doubts, and give in to their old patterns, which accompany them from before. But it still needs to be said that everything needs its opposite. Positive energy also needs its negative, so we know what positive energy is like. Every positive atom needs its negative atom, the night needs light, the sun needs rain, and everything needs its opposite, so we know what is positive. When we feel the minus, the negative, we know how we feel and what the positive is like. So when you become aware, try to move the negative into the positive. That is when you make the decision and move like this:

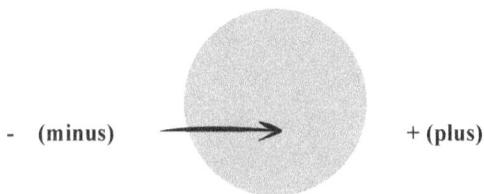

- (minus) ⟶ + (plus)

This is the big thing I'm telling you. You are not always aware of the positive, so whenever you find yourself on the negative point (the minus), you must choose JOY once more to raise your point of vibration. That is all it takes. Decide to slowly change your minuses in all the areas of your life into pluses. A beautiful game that will help you live.

Live the game, don't die!

Your God.

"It's not hard to see the truth when the heart is open. It's written like an open book."

22nd message: TEN MOST IMPORTANT "INGREDIENTS" OF A PERSON'S LIFE

Before one of the next channelized messages, I asked God to briefly tell me which are the most important "ingredients" of a person's life in ten bullets. He told me that the life cycle when a person is working out of love is as follows:

1. LOVE

2. JOY

3. HAPPINESS

4. FULFILLMENT

5. BEAUTY – BEING BEAUTIFUL

6. LIGHT – TO BE BRIGHT

7. RADIANCE – TO SHINE BRIGHT

8. ALLOWING and RECEIVING

9. MANIFESTATION

10. Out of LOVE, LIGHT, and RADIANCE, to FULFILLMENT through RECEIVING and to MANIFESTATION of all forms of PLENTY.

"There are no smart decisions, only big ones and small ones. It is up to you how you decide and what each decision will bring."

23rd message: DO NOT STAIN YOUR CELLS WITH WORRY

Dear Sandra,

My angel, today we will write about the most important subject on this planet, **carefreeness**. When a person is carefree and without worry, he is open to all ideas, the greatest shining innovations – that is when within them lives a pure, beautiful energy full of light, and in their heads the most beautiful thoughts. That is when they are not worried, not feeling cowardly, and they act without worry.

Do you understand what I'm trying to tell you? When we do not worry, we are open to love, beautiful things, and the light that shines and lives above us in the entirety of its divinity. That is when we are connected to God because God does not create fear and worry. God only loves you.

Write a book, look in the mirror, and create the good energy of creation that births new ideas and innovation lives within you when you are carefree. It's beautiful seeing a person who is full of ideas. But those only come when we are carefree.

When worry is not on our minds. Why even worry? Worry is a type of fear or insecurity, something that does not come from you and is an illusion. Worry in most cases does not come true, does it?

How many times were you worried that you were going to be late for work? But were you late? You weren't. See, worry is just another form of fear that threads your mind. When you're worried, the cells in your mind cannot operate and don't know how to be in charge and make decisions. That is when you make irrelevant, unwise decisions that only lead you into more worry.

But who can help when you are worried? No one. You must help yourself because you are the one who creates worry in your head. Instead of your head saying: "Hey, everything will be alright, it will all settle itself in the end," you fill your little head with worry with the thought: "What now? Oh how will I do this and how will I do that, this won't end well, I don't have enough money, I'm going to be too late, they'll chase me down the dark street, I can't pay my bills, I worry about my health, oh no, this hurts so much, I can't do this, I don't know how to do this, does he even love me, I don't know if I'll be late to class, I don't know what I'm going to eat today there's nothing in the fridge and so on…"

Ah, and oh and ugh: do you see how much worry you people throw into that stained thinking gold mine in your head? What good comes from this unhealthy mine of black thoughts that daily pushes you into even greater worry, doubt, and fear?

No good. So, please, people, be different. Worry will only bring you even greater worry; it will suffocate you, choke you by the neck, and weaken your immune system. And then after the worry comes a million and one other diseased states because your cells are dying piecemeal and are breaking down like an old car that is just beyond help. Do you know what worry and worried thoughts do?

Look at this cell, let me draw it for you:

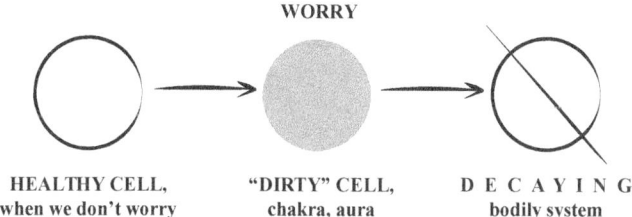

WORRY

HEALTHY CELL,
when we don't worry

"DIRTY" CELL,
chakra, aura

D E C A Y I N G
bodily system

Do you see? The cell, which is pure because it is the master of full, beautiful, and carefree thoughts, is pure and clean. Clean. Clean as a tear. It would be even better if we drew it as a tear because it is like a cell, pure, just like this:

But then you begin to worry: "Oh no, woe is me, I can't do this, it hurts, but what's going to happen if I... What do I do now? Oh no, I can't do this... I'll be late, oh no, it's happening again... What do I do now?!" Oh my, a thousand and one worries just in one day. And that beautiful tear is already a little stained after just one day.

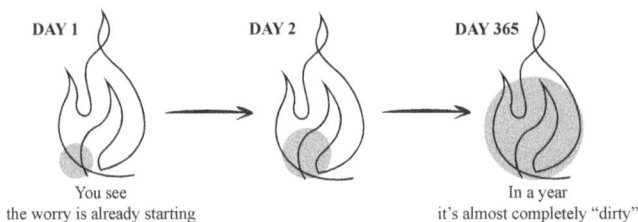

That's what happens with just one cell, but in your body, my dear friends, there are trillions. And in one year, you stain each one through and through with your worries. Where else are all your insecurities, your doubts? Oh, better not count them all.

FEAR + INSECURITY + WORRY + DOUBT =

Your decaying body leads you into diseased states of one kind or another. This leads to you being filled with sickness, flying from doctor to doctor, and getting medicine to solve all of your medical issues.

94

But what do I, God, give you? All the time I'm giving you divine love, which is already inside of you. It is inside, my dear friends! But you do not see it, and you do not choose it. You'd rather take **worry**, weave it up, and place it atop your head so your entire body starts to ache. Why? Because you choose to.

Every day, 365 days a year. Let me tell you right now that you don't have to. It's all within yourself already, my dear friends, all the things you need and often look for outside yourself, you forget are already there within yourself. Your divinity, your plenty, plenty of everything: Health, beauty, harmony, happiness, love, money, beautiful relationships... Whatever you want is already abundant within every single one of you, in the core of your very being, body, mind, and spirit. Just seize it and have it. Do not look for it outside, away from yourself.

The radiance (God calls it "the whiteness") is not created when you think God is creating it for you. The radiant white light is already deep within you. Do not stain it like you do a plain apron in the kitchen. Take care of it, keep it, maintain it, take it with you always, and let it serve you on your life's journey. I cannot ignore the fact that you are sometimes taught wrong: Your environment and the entire hierarchical system teach you and often stain your radiance. Avoid this trap and give yourself into your own hands and be who you are. God-given. Pure, beautiful, and fearless. Carefree pretty people, with a pure and lovely karmic soul, who expect nothing but love.

Your God.

"Sensing beauty is like a sunbeam peeking out from behind the clouds. If beauty is not there, the cloud also cannot work, but if it is, the cloud identifies with the rainbow."

24th message: WORRY AND IMPURE THOUGHTS TAKE YOU AWAY FROM DIVINITY

Dear angel,

My Sandra, take in as much of my beauty and take it to the world. Let me work through you and be your guide.

So, let us write something about the depth of carefree thoughts–thoughts that are not wandering in the dark, but are as pure as spring water. These are the beautiful thoughts you should be saving up in your beautiful little heads all day. What does your beautiful head say when you fill it up with bright, beautiful, positive, and radiant thoughts? It is happy. Your head is overjoyed. Let's not even talk about your mind… Now think of something beautiful and feel it. Let's say that you have a partner whom you've recently fallen head over heels for. What are you feeling right now? What do you feel? I'm telling you, I'm asking you about what you feel when thinking about the partner you've fallen in love with, and who's also fallen for you?

Something incredibly beautiful, right? You're overcome by a magical wave of love. There's a chemical reaction triggering within you that jump-starts everything inside your body into health. When you think about how much you love your partner, husband, or child, you are as blessed. A state of pure bliss, right? You're overcome by a feeling of beauty, peace, happiness, and indescribable joy, and harmony begins to come alive inside you. But do you know what this means for you? Plenty! At that moment, that beautiful thought – let's say the husband you love so much and you've woken up next to and made love to him – releases inside of you an immeasurable beautiful feeling of calm and pure love. This feeling, this beautiful feeling, like you people say, infuses the entire body, hugs all of your chakras, and sends you on your way toward even more positive energy. All of this, my friends, happens in your beautiful body.

That is how one beautiful thought interacts with your body when you feel it. This feeling triggers a wave of chemical reactions in your body that beneficially affect every cell, organ, and tissue in your body. It's all a process, my friends. A process you create every day, every minute, and every second. With just one thought! In the beginning, I said we are going to be talking about a well, the countless thoughts drenching you every day, and the 365 days in a year that comprise your calendar.

So you see, my friends, what on a physical level one beautiful thought and its connected emotions do inside your body? What would happen if even more of these feelings, coming from these many beautiful thoughts, continued to appear? It would be perfect. Your body would be in a state of perfect health. Your body would not become sick, and you would not become ill. Do you wish to be sick and have immense issues with your health? No. Of course not. I hear this from you all the time, my friends.

But you say: "But I don't want to be sick! God, you've abandoned us, you allowed us to be sick! We're angry at you, God, because you left us in disease, because you allowed us to be sick. God, you are nothing, we don't believe in you anymore because you allow us good people to be ravaged by disease!" I hear this all the time from you. But I'm telling you, even though it might be better if I yell:

"I have not abandoned you, you have abandoned yourself, people. When you separate yourself from me and leave me, because you are no longer ONE with me, that is why you became sick. I am not the one who abandoned you, but you who abandoned me. I am always inside of you because you are the spark and embodiment of my love. So do not leave, my dear friends. This is a message I always try to give to you – you have left me, and so you fell into sickness and disease!"

Do you understand me? By leaving me, you separate yourself from me. When you are separated from me, my friends, you are no longer with me. And when you are apart from me, you are not in love with me or yourself. Because when you think impure thoughts and you are worried and afraid, you are not connected with me, but separated, as you have abandoned me.

And then, my friends, what I just said happens to you. You dirty your mind, emotions, and feelings, and this results in your diseases. So, my friends, come back and connect with yourself, with me, find me and say: "Thank you, God, I'm coming back to you, I wish to be connected with you, I wish us to be one!" Only then can you be in touch with my divinity, with the divine love, which will give you beautiful and positive thoughts that will connect you to yourself. You will not get sick as your body will be infused with health, healthy feelings, and a yearning, shivering clamoring for the pure divinity.

Your God.

"Alluring are the flowers that bloom on a meadow full of love."

25th message: CONNECT TO THE TRAIN WE CALL GOD

Why do people think that their soul is somehow separate from them? Why do these thoughts creep into their mind? It is because their thoughts are not divine, and have detached from the train we call God. Can you imagine it? The God-train.

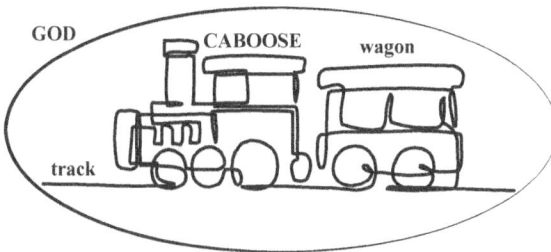

Do not laugh, my dear friends! God is everything, and **God is with everything**. You are God, as is everyone and all creation. As your carriage is attached and holding on to the engine, it rolls nicely and comfortably along the beautiful and peaceful path. But when one wagon becomes detached, it leaves the path, ventures out on its own, and no longer travels on the God-given path, and is separated from the God-given energy. You see, that is when the wagon goes off on its own, it derails and doesn't follow the established God-given paths and tracks, but separates itself, no longer one, going out on its own! It goes and separates from God. That is when it goes astray.

That is you, my friends, when you stray, when you lose me, when you as the wagon, venture out on your own and derail, and then - BOOM - life no longer seems as it should! With this comes crying, stress, sadness, the devil's sickness, and finally death!

Hold on to the engine, my friends, because only with its help and guidance will the divine path be clear. It knows the way and knows the path. A wagon detached can only stray as it doesn't know the path and so gets lost. Lost, afraid, in doubt, and filled with dark and negative emotions, it worries about the way ahead.

But perhaps the train engine rolls by again and grabs the wagon one more time.

And it does grab it. It grabs the wagon again and asks: »Are you coming along, little one? Hold on to me and my divinity, and let's travel together again along my divine path that is always there for you. Are you coming? Hop along and grab on tight! «

And God winks at you. God is here again, saving you. Jumping on with glee, you're back with him. Connected, on the divine path, facing life head-on, as life comes to you. But most of you, my friends, remain lonely and derailed, cautiously lying by the path you could have driven on with the engine, and yet you decide not to grab on. The whole thing is as simple as it is always within reach. So come to my friends, grab on and ride with me. I know the way, the divine path of life.

Your God.

"Don't close the door behind you, as every door always leads somewhere where you'll find your goals and your paths of love."

19th September 2019

26th message: OPEN YOURSELF FOR THE MESSAGES FROM THE KINGDOM OF HEAVEN

Dear Sandra,

My angel, let us tell the world today how happy and joyful I am to see that people are daily becoming more and more aware that their life depends on their dreams, expectations, and actions. But I still wish to talk about everything that still needs doing to make the world a true heavenly paradise. Our heavenly kingdom continuously warns people about the invisible and visible signs by sending messages to people. When people are in crisis, we, God, angels, archangels, and divine assistants, help them see the signs. We wish to tell them that all will be alright and that everything's already alright, that they can rely on me and the heavenly beings that watch over them from high above, our heavenly abode.

What should people do when they're in crisis? They should ask for help. If they do not ask for help, we cannot help, we cannot intervene. Our task is not to guide people to do something or tell them how to choose in a given situation, but to always provide help when it's called on. When they wish for help from us. Then, we heavenly beings are obliged to help the people of Earth. That is when we are there to show you the path. So my dear friends, call upon us and tell us what crisis you're in and what is bothering you.

We will **help** you! We will send messages in the form of signs, messages, numbers, heavenly signs, shapes of clouds, rain, sun, calls…There are innumerable paths we can reveal, signs we can give that you are on the right path. You will receive a sign that all is well. That everything will be ok and that you are not alone. Can you hear me? You will always receive comfort; you will know we are there and that you are not alone. Things will become easier, as we will comfort you the way a mother soothes her child.

So what must you do, my dear friends? Firstly, please ask for help; secondly, be open to receiving and seeing signs and messages we send – allow yourself to see, hear, feel, and sense; thirdly, interpret and try to read the message and give it meaning and value – think, what the sign actually means to you. These three steps are important for you, my friends, if you wish for divine guidance:

1. **ASK** for help, call us, talk to us, yell into the sky. Write it down, dance it, or just say out loud what troubles you. You can call us through dancing, you can sit quietly and just speak softly, you can look into the sky and pray. Whatever feels right to you. Just call us and ask for help.

2. **ALLOW** yourself to hear, see, and feel the signs we send. Notice them, be observant, and sense them.

3. **READ** our messages when you sense them. Try to decode them and you will be unburdened.

Maybe you will receive it through a song you suddenly hear on the radio, maybe this song will sound like intuition in your ears and suddenly you will begin to sing it; maybe you will see certain numbers, which will tell you what to do in a certain situation; you might see a cloud in the shape of an angel (or some other sign in the sky); perhaps you will receive some other intuitive message. We will always comfort you and show you that you are never alone in a given situation, and will, through your intuition, signs, messages, sightings, and the reading of messages, show you that you are on the right path and what to do. These are angelic and divine messages that accompany you all the time. I, my angels, constantly communicate with you, but most of you do not perceive us, or fail to see us. We message you all the time when we see your requests and prayers for help. We are here all the time. But you must call us and then follow our messages.

It's very important that you eventually become more and more open to all the messages that my angels and I use to communicate with you. By cleansing your channels, you will achieve this greater clarity, clairvoyance, sixth sense, and clarity of purpose. But to become more and more open, you must clean your channels if they are stained. In the same way, you can't cook a good dinner in a dirty pan, you can't receive our messages when the channels you use to receive are stained and dirty.

Through meditation and a meditative state, clean the channels up, so they will be clean and ready to receive clearer messages! You will achieve this with a cleaner crown chakra, as well as all the others. To connect with us, you must be clean, radiant, and divine. You see, this divinity is always present within yourself when you wish to achieve something in your life.

Whether something is achievable is always conditioned on whether you are in a state of divinity or not. Unattached from God and in a state that does not allow divinity, it becomes very difficult to live and to give ourselves to anything. Our actions are always dependent on our decisions. Our decisions will always be right and immeasurably good when we are divine! That is when we accept God's leadership in the form and way we easily recognize. That is why we make decisions based on whether we are latched onto the train.

Meditation should be a key component of your life. You do not have to meditate like the gurus; just go into nature, and there you will already feel the peace and harmony, which will take you into a meditative state. Close your eyes, watch the plants, and calm your mind as this truly calms the soul and weaves you into the web of your dreams and expectations. The peaceful environment then enables your soul to begin partial manifestation. Your meditation can, of course, be even deeper. You can choose any form of meditation that will awaken you from your stressful state and return you to balance, like a conditioner for your hair. You can't expect to be open to the signs of God when your auras and chakras are dirty and stained, as they cannot work and properly channel the energy of the universe as they were meant to. Be mindful of this as it is very important when you wish to hear, see, feel, and simply know what God and his angels are trying to tell you.

The fact is that your nature does not always allow the necessary state needed to reinvigorate the spirit and perform meditative exercises, however, you can always take at least **10 minutes** a day. This will strengthen your sleep, your soul will be better prepared to channel the big things, and you will be open to divine leadership, the way the channel in Venice guides the waters.

Your God.

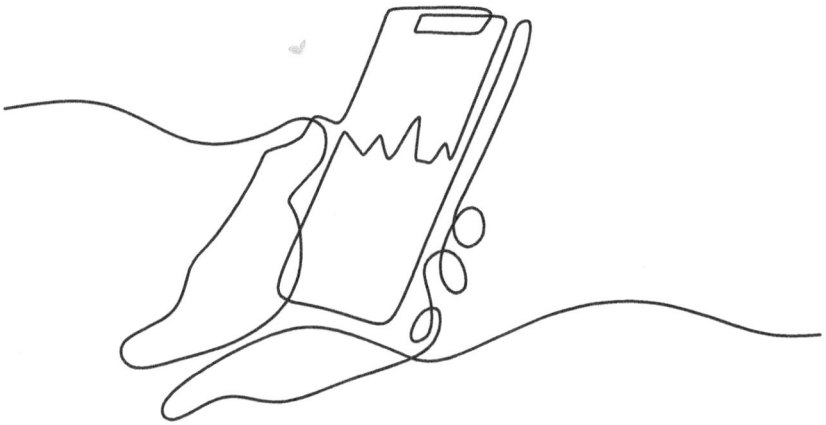

"Drive away thoughts not fit for purpose. The beautiful, pure thoughts of endless love, these are the ones that give you wings."

23rd September 2019

27th message: TECHNOLOGICAL INTOXICATION TAKES YOU AWAY FROM DIVINITY

Dear Sandra,

My angel, let us today say something about the weaknesses that modern life brings with it. What drives a person to spend all their time with their phone and computer, attached to them and separated from themselves, and alienated from the flow of divinity and divine energy. A car can't work and drive if we close the gas tank, can it? I don't think so. Open the faucet, people, and see what you can do when you see your life in crisis. Modern technologies take you away from nature, that true authenticity, beauty, and richness that enriches your spirit and soul. The soul does not imagine a daily struggle with resolutions that do not belong in its world, mind, and spirit. The greatest inventions have always come when the soul is singing. *"Singing in the Rain"* landed on the biggest and most exposed shelf in the bookstore and is sung by people around the world. The mind is at rest, then as the soul and spirituality work for the whole.

You will come nearer to the situations you wish to achieve by not punishing yourself and others. By staying away from all the phone numbers that distract you throughout the day and brainwash your head in impure ways. The way you will log off is something your heart and soul will tell you. To thank the greatest giant for his achievements in the telecommunication space is worthless and will not enrich the soul. The soul does not sing when it is in the grip of instant messages, telephone calls, playing games, and constant flirting with computers. These play with the mind and not the soul. When we are relaxed and do things for ourselves, the system of the soul is not subjected to situations that drag us down. Why do you think that the guru's "guru" lies on beautiful cots, stretches, and does yoga? Because they do not have phones and do not need to constantly stare at a screen and send messages. They do not even want to see the phone up close. Their nature is what fulfills them and makes the phone calls within their souls. They sing songs to destroy the greatest grime that constantly falls off them.

Do not worry about money in this case, because your income will not drop if you are tied to an activity, because this is not a priority in your life. Your life will start to flow when you stop your horses for a bit and relax in nature, feel the different comfort disconnected from the constant thinking about what business you still need to do, the constant staring into a screen, phone, and other technological things of intoxication.

These things get you drunk the same way alcohol does a drunk. You no longer know how to be happy without these shiny, electronic gadgets that make you stupid and disconnected from the world and yourself.

Why allow a phone to blind and enslave you? Why not do all the other great, beautiful things that bring you health, and success, and improve your intelligence, instead of crawling through Google, looking at your phone directory, working on computerized data, and delving into a world that does not serve you?

For a little while, delve into something that makes you happy. Singing by yourself, or maybe in a quire, dancing, or maybe even crafting great culinary delights. There you knead, dance, sing, and obtain beautiful energy, which takes you down a different path. This way you connect with yourself and with the energy of the divine. Divinity can only be created like this and never with new, advanced technological gadgets. Your being is just one, and it will allow you to exploit it until all you have left is more and more of these technological vices, which grab you, intoxicate you, and exploit you. And they are also expensive. They will bring you nothing good, besides the few moments of fun you'll feel with your eyes darting across the screen of these technological creations. Do not be ashamed to admit that you constantly type on your phone while you're doing things that you love doing (which ones?), but this takes you to the other world, which is not divine.

A car needs to be fueled by the correct gasoline, as a diesel needs diesel, so too does your body need its true nutrition. Let your faith and choice be natural, God-given, and always authentic.

Your God.

"Through beauty, you can travel far, very far."

28th message: THE MORE YOU GIVE, THE MORE YOU HAVE

Sympathetic creation that wants to understand is always the best. When you try to understand the actions of your fellow man, you are led by the impulse of creation. At that moment, you're not wondering what's right and wrong. You know exactly what's right for you and what isn't. At that point, you don't do unreasonable things, you're not writing bad words, and are not eating fast food, in that moment your heart is writing a story written up in heaven, in divinity. When you understand yourself, you come from yourself and the understanding that you are worthy, that you are beautiful, that you like yourself, that you love yourself, and so caress yourself every day. But it's an even more beautiful situation when you understand others because this also leads the one you understand into a state of beauty. That is when the circle of mutual understanding is complete, and we can mark this circle as a beautiful love, a love that heals.

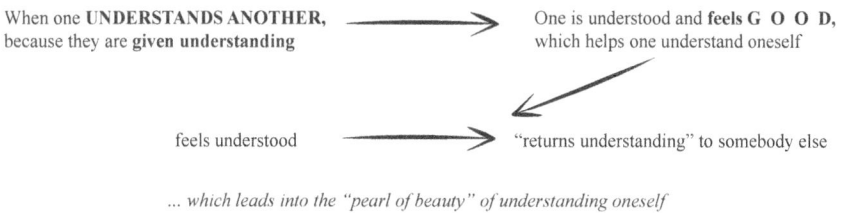

When one **UNDERSTANDS ANOTHER,**
because they are **given understanding** ⟶ One is understood and **feels G O O D,** which helps one understand oneself

feels understood ⟶ "returns understanding" to somebody else

... which leads into the "pearl of beauty" of understanding oneself

Like a circular flow, isn't it? But what happens when this flow stops? When does it only run in one direction? When no one understands themselves or those around them? That is when the flow, which could lead our understanding to a higher level, stops. The person is then unable to receive divine energy, much less give it out. For the flow to once again flow in both directions, one must act quickly and work on oneself. One must look in the mirror and say: *"What do you, human, want to understand, so that your soul can sing and I can understand myself?"*

And when one finds the answer, one becomes aware that they are a winner. The person then understands themselves and can also understand others. The flow once again goes both ways. The other soul feels understood and so focuses on its understanding. The other soul then returns the understanding to the first because they now beautifully understand themselves.

A world like that is filled with more beauty and understanding, and it takes us high into the sky. We feel good, which also affects the beauty of all other people and the entire earth. Do not be afraid to be understood and to understand others. It is like two jewels we carry in the side pockets. Occasionally, we give them a little tap to remind ourselves that they're there. Is there anything wrong if we don't feel them constantly? The important thing is that we know they're there and that we can touch them. It's then that we feel that joy that carries us into the higher spheres, spheres of light and divinity. I don't know why people do not wish to wear and keep two jewels in their pockets as if someone will steal them from them. But they will not, no one can steal them while they're snug in the corner of your pockets and remind us that they're there.

Bring your passion and leave your bias on the other side; leave it at home. Feel the two gems and head out into the wide world as a gem smith. The world will be glad for it, and you will also be glad for it. Because you will give and you will receive. **And the more you give, the more you receive.** Remember?

you give more

$$\downarrow \uparrow$$

you have more, you get more

A kind of mathematical potency that never fades when used. Do not write it down, use it. Every day, you will joyously turn the arrows at all levels of your life: in your relationships, love, joy, business, greatest events, all of that which you call life. The joy of life will draw out a well you've always wanted to put into the middle of your home and playground.

Your God.

"What lies within you is your POWER."

29th message: FEAR IS NOTHING, BUT YOU FEEL IT STRONG

Dear Sandra,

My dear angel, the best stories are born in the greatest joy. I wish for you, Sandra, my dear, to be my angel forever and to share light in the world. So write down what I will say to you.

I'm sure you all know what **fear** is. That hollow cavity, the void that expands around your head every time you think you need to think fearful thoughts. It is a feeling of hollowness, a feeling of unique fearful misfortune that makes you act like a machine that cannot be pulled either left or right. The chasm between your fearful thoughts and the re-establishment of your beautiful thoughts is vast. As vast as the Grand Canyon. At that moment, your cells and molecules don't know how to act, are constantly afraid that they will die, and finally say goodbye to their days of being. Why does this happen?

Because you feel a fearful separation from your being and your true roots. Roots that are different from what you think. It was due to the greatest creations that the world had no fear because people then were not acting out of fear, but out of faith, science, beauty, thoughts of success, and beautiful moments strewn about with flowers. The greatest creations did not come about from a fearful mind. Let's take it one at a time.

What is fear? Nothing, absolutely nothing. Zero. A timeless space of nothing. That which you do not see but very strongly feel as something ugly, negative, black, penetrating, and invisible, but always veiled by a veneer of secrecy.

What to do with it when it pounces? Nothing, you will say, what can you do? Oh, but you can. Sprinkle it like dust all around yourself, and you will see that you will not be helped. You will want to leave, go to sleep, and wrap yourself in the coat of inequality and terror while the life meant for you goes who knows where. So write down what I'm telling you.

Your evil thoughts turn into beautiful, pure thoughts. That is the first step to at least lessen the feeling of fear you're feeling for a little bit. You can't just leave. Fear infuses you, and you become tangled up in a ball that's strangling you with the thinnest thread. It cuts your neck and suffocates you. But is it necessary? Not at all. You're allowing yourself to be bound by this rope, this noose. You walk as if your steps are not your own, as if being pushed from behind and being followed. As if someone is about to push you down into the depths. That is what fear does. Exactly what it does. But why? Because this is the feeling you sense when you so decide and do not wish to let go. But why is the light inside yourself turned off? Is it gone? It could have been gone for days, weeks, months, or years; perhaps the light has been off your entire life, and so fear grips you, grabs you, and chokes you as stated before.

Does it feel nice to be choked? Well, of course not! You blew it, you are living and creating black thoughts. Thoughts which are not your own. They are not your own at all. It is foolish to think that you will be able to save anything like this, very foolish indeed. Drop the fear, breathe in, bend over, close your eyes, lie down, or whatever it is you wish to do to take a step back. A step back from the fear. It will not give you true happiness, but this one step will make the burden of fear slightly easier to bear. Like a drop in the ocean separated from the sea, yet the sea remains! Look, your judgments, your lifestyle, your fear, your cowardice, all of this makes you

118

unhappy and leads you to taste eternal disloyalty and restlessness. Instead, drink from the well of joy. A happy life is within reach, but you will not allow it in.

Except for empathy, I do not know what could overcome your mind more than fear. This is not a joke you tell at a bar; these are real debates about the greatest happiness you're not experiencing. Imagine you are somewhere where no one can find you. You wish to be found because you've fallen into a hole. Fear is like the devil. What will you do? Wait in the hole to be found? Cry like the never-ending rain and feel sorry for yourself? Ask yourself why you've fallen into the hole. Why, why, why? Or will you turn the page and start a new story?

Will you try to somehow get outside the hole? Will you grab the rocks and climb out of the hole? What do you think is better, to think and be stuck inside with your hands full of fear, or letting the fear go and somehow get to the top and get out of this devilish hole? Think about what you'd like more.

I would leave. But you, I don't know.

I see too many people every day who cry inside their hole, unable to get out. And it takes so little. Only the light inside yourself, only divinity from which you've removed yourself and are thus being dragged back into the hole. The hole where there is nothing, nothing but fear. Nothing else. Give yourself another light and dig yourself out of your everyday pits of fear, which frighten you and offer you nothing good.

There are too many good things in this world that belong to you. Good food, a nice bed, beautiful jobs, beautiful cars, beautiful things. But you refuse to take them and simply do not wish to pick them up. They lie in front of your threshold, ready for the taking, but your conscious mind is always looking for fear and other worries, which drag you away from the door. It would be best if you stopped this cycle. This is not your life; this is your despair and your inability to fight back against all of these frightfully bad thoughts and situations.

Revelation is key. You must reveal to yourself what you really want. Do you want fear or your perfect life in all its manifesting forms? Do not leave the page unwritten because of fear. Do not leave it unwritten because you are godless, lazy, and unhappy about the things you do not have. Own the fear, throw it away, and learn to work as if the divine radiant hand is guiding and infusing you every day. Your greatest treasure lies inside of you. It leads you to a fulfilled life, filled with goodness and plenty. The best thing to do is to soak yourself in love. Love yourself and others, and keep traveling the path with the train. Remember the train I was talking to you about? Come, latch your wagon to it, and take a ride into a world of imagination, which is more than just imagination, but the life you wish and deserve to live.

Your God.

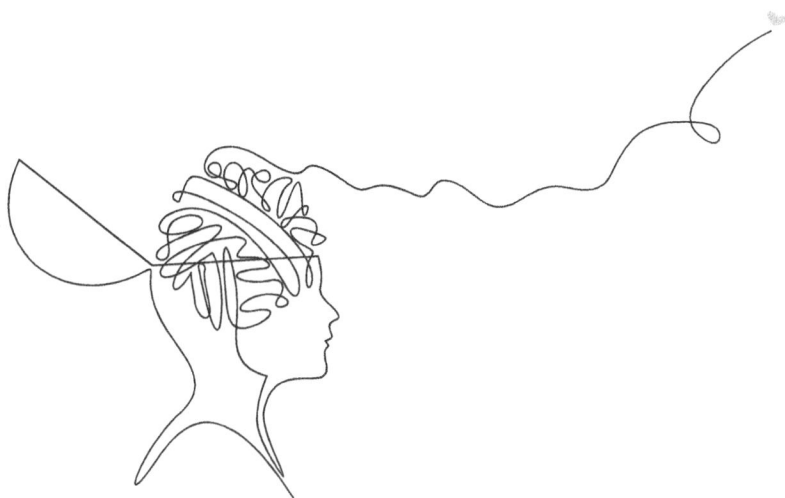

"Love is the Guide with all things in life.
Let it not be forgotten and never thrown away.
Let it always be present within every action in your life. "

30th message: EGO – THE WORMY, PARASITIC CREATURE, THAT BURROWS IN US ALL

Dear Sandra,

My angel, I'm talking to you to write down my words. Why do people not read more, instead watching more and more ballast on television; torture themselves with crime stories, which make them even more nervous, and are not tackling life as spiritual creatures?

You know, Sandra, you made sure to be our spiritual being. Man is first and foremost a spiritual being, with all the rest coming after that. Because of human tendencies towards ego, more and more people are afraid to embrace spirituality and accept it as a given.

Writing is one thing, but the other side of life is living. We most often expend ourselves when we talk from our ego. Egoism is a way of functioning that leads a person to creation not in the here and now. Here and now means an endless ease of living, which unfolds based on the rules of the true soul. The soul never calls the ego living here and now. The soul then sings and does not long for ego. That desperate, wormy, parasitic creature that burrows in us and leads us into despair, fear, uncertainty, and movement of the body that feeds on it day to day. The head isn't clean, then, doing things out of desperation and feeling sorry for itself. Emotions become threaded by negativity and intoxicating substances like alcohol, drugs, and addictions of every kind.

Before continuing, listen to that little voice I call **intuition**. Do you perchance know that little voice, my dear friends? Eternally knocking on the door of your mind and heart, trying to tell you that you are beautiful, wise, cool, and the greatest driver of the life you want to know how to drive.

I think giving you the metaphor of the sun will bring the most happiness to you.

A sun that shines and doesn't go behind the clouds. A sun that shines and gives beautiful sunny energy that should be like you and your beautiful souls. Sometimes you need to tell the ego loudly to stop its egoistic stepping out and look the soul in the eyes. Beautiful, heartfelt eyes are always ready for the beauty of each passing day.

When you argue and yell, you're only thinking more and more, and thus feeding your ego with the sweetest bread it likes. But you should bake good bread with the label of love and feed the ego. You'll see him fall asleep and quiet down like a little child when full.

The beautiful words of the great master who feels the most unrest will turn into a cohesive whole surrounded by a thousand bottom-dwelling water lilies, and the nonsense will be carved out. Carve into the greatest well of jokes and the greatest humor. Behind the chair, you'll find a leaflet, which will talk about just this and will teach you that you have nothing to look for if you're not sleeping in a bed that is not yours.

What your head will say at that time, you can just think. Mostly because your mind will not allow bleached jokes without the allowance of the other side. Like it or not, you're going to have to tell yourself that you are living for yourself and are responsible for your actions. You cannot get past this without the ego grabbing hold of you again, so try to quiet it down.

Calm down your mind and tackle it. Like with boxing, which nobody likes. Things can be controlled the same way here, except you cannot take it anymore. You need to leave your comfort zone, but because you can't, you're trying to catch yourself. Like a cat hunts a mouse when the master isn't home.

And this angers you horribly because you are not on the pedestal of happiness and satisfaction, but are wandering in the darkened shadow of space, an otherwise very nice place. Between you and your head is a great chasm, which you refuse to jump across due to your ego.

Travel into the unknown, perhaps it will be better, perhaps it will suit you better.

The most beautiful stories will be written when you love. Love is the one that destroys the ego and drives it to the great beyond, never to be seen again. Just try to bring it to your lips as longing, and you'll fall into the same noose of complications. To finish, I wish to give you all a saying:

"Last chances are always the ones most wanted, because you realize that they will never come again, and yet you still cling to the still seething ego awakening inside you, everything but love."

You wear your head like it is for sale and do not wish to change. Only your brave ego knows why you are doing this. As I said, let it go, capture it in a closed cup of human elusiveness and you will win. You'll be left with the last chance to get back up, to raise your hands towards the sky and exclaim "Hurrah!". You're the winner. Is that so hard? Now let me just say one more thought.

Write it down:

"THE STONE NOT THROWN REMAINS WITH YOU. GUARD IT, DO NOT WAKE THE EGO AND JEALOUSY INSIDE AND IT WILL STAY WITH YOU FOREVER."

Your God.

"What you think you are, you attract. Do not be afraid to think beautiful thoughts. They are liberating."

31st message: THE HEART IS LIKE A BOOK. OPEN IT AND DON'T WRITE CRIME NOVELS!

Let your word today be pure; purity is that which keeps the world white, beautiful, and bountiful in the sense of love. It never dies, it does not hide, does not escape, if your heart is open. How many closed hearts have I seen! People, open them. Sandra is bringing you the message, which will spread around the world, and with ships sailing around it.

Bursting books will reach you in sprawling cities and are just this text, which will work through every letter like a cure. At night, put this book, full of love and pure health, underneath your pillow, beside your pillow, keep it open, and let your head through the night weave together the words of healing through this book.

Let happiness never leave you, not even at night when it's dark, when your dreams and the greatest ravishing horns come to visit your beautiful dreams. Do you still remember what dreams are? They are your indicator of what will be, what has been, and what your heart thinks about your life on earth.

You cannot fool your heart, as it is like a Viking in his armor, working and fighting for you. What you give to him out of your mind is what he gets, and that is also what you get back, my dears. How many of you think about how your heart is doing every day? And I'm not talking physically, but how it's feeling and whether it's doing what it knows. I mean, what does it **FEEL**! Yes, what does it FEEL? Have you ever asked yourself? How is your heart doing? What does it feel like? You haven't, you very rarely do this. Do it, people! I command you. Get up in the morning and ask yourself:

"Hello, my lovely heart, how do you feel? Now that we're up, what are you FEELING? Will we do things today so that I will feel the nice and beautiful feelings of happiness and joy, or will we be ruthless and torture you again with all the old agonies and uncomfortableness?"

That is how you begin. Ask it. It will tell you everything it needs to tell you. Do not give it vain negative situations, because it hates that. It gets tired and quickly gets sick. But not from arrhythmia or other heart conditions, but from a lack of love. That crushes it. That is why it dies.

My darlings, the heart is like a book. If within it you write poetry and songs, it will sing. But if you write crime novels it will be poor. So do not write crime novels but write songs. Songs about love. About eternal love to yourself, living beings, the world, and your own heart.

It will undoubtedly lead you to a place, where you will not write poetry and songs, but crime novels. In those times, be a singer that writes crime songs. I'm joking, a little joke. But, really now. That is when you open up, clean up the wound in your heart that was created while writing the crime novel, and begin to heal that wound. It will be grateful to you, your heart will begin pumping and working at 100 hertz. It will be happy and you will be happy.

Now come with me.

Your God.

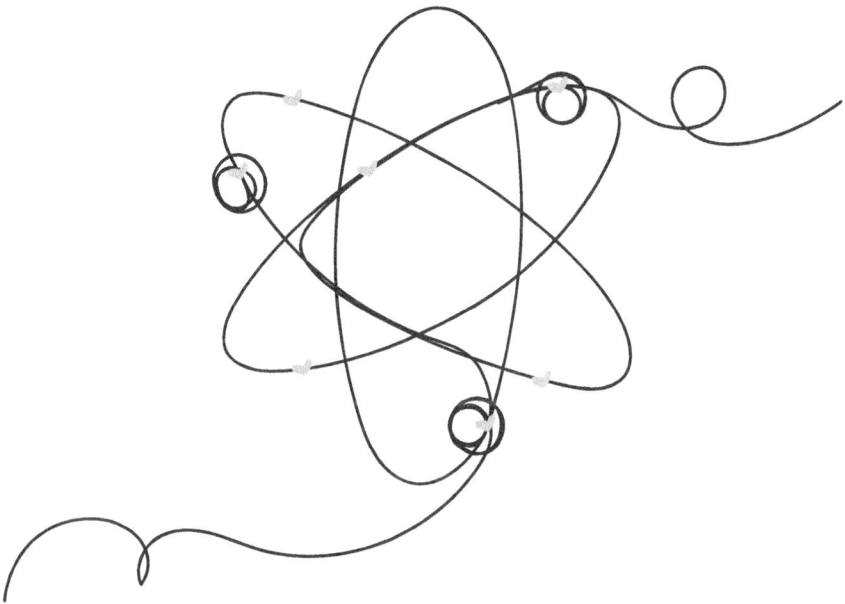

"Building relationships is priceless. Be the best bricklayer and have the best material."

32nd message: THE ATOMS OF LOVE AND THE CLOSED-OFF HEART

The flames of love are always burning when the heart is open. Let me connect to my previous message about a heart and its openness. People always think that their hearts is too heavy to receive love. But it is not so. The heart is always connected to the great divinity, to me, and it is always open. I've been repeating this throughout the entire text of this book. It can never close if you do not do it first, and if you people don't make it so. It is always open to plenty, to beautiful relationships, and divine plenty in all of its forms.

What drives a person to close off their heart? Their actions stem from their ego, their greatest chasm of shameful desires, where there is nothing but shame, guilt, fear, lack of plenty, and unsavory people. That is the only way they close the valve on their heart, which always closes them off from all and everyone who wishes good for them. Doomsday doesn't mean that love is lost. It is always there. Everywhere, in the smallest atom, even when we're sleeping, when we make love, when we talk, when we go for a visit, and when we play cat and mouse.

Do you know what the smallest atom of love looks like? Like this:

These are the small atoms of love that are present everywhere, every second, and every moment our heart is open. And when open, they are here within us like tiny rocks in a mosaic. But when it is closed, these beautiful atoms of love are gone. That's when the picture looks like this:

Empty heart with nothing in it, not even an atom of love

So, I tell you what to do to make the atoms stay there all the time. Because they are there all the time. Don't let them disappear, don't let them leave, to wisp away, only you can drive them from your heart circle.

Go into nature as much as you can, because this Gaia, Earth, is woven with beautiful nature, giving you all wings. Then listen to yourself in nature: sit, stand, move, close your eyes, and **listen to your heart**! Stop, mentally relax your thoughts, and feel at home: let every moment be here and now, and listen to what your heart is telling you. Ask it: "What do you feel, WHAT DO YOU FEEL, my darling heart?"

Then recognize all of your emotions. Don't analyze them. Only feel them. If these feelings are bad, full of longing after bad, and something that is not yours but someone else's, recognize them. Recognize them in all their size, color, and shade, and then try to – I said try to – let go! Try to let go of these negative and ugly feelings. Let them go away. Let them leave your heart. That is when your heart will sense and feel some other feelings, which will return life to your heart and joy, beauty, and love to you.

But if your heart is filled with beautiful feelings, then just raise your head up, lean against your shoulder, and congratulate yourself on the most beautiful feelings, which are leading you into a beautiful, heart-filled world. That is life, my darlings. When you feel that you have everything. This is the love that fills your heart with the little atoms of love that sneak inside your heart. Or were there all along, if your thoughts and feelings were full of love. Then you just breathe in life.

Your God.

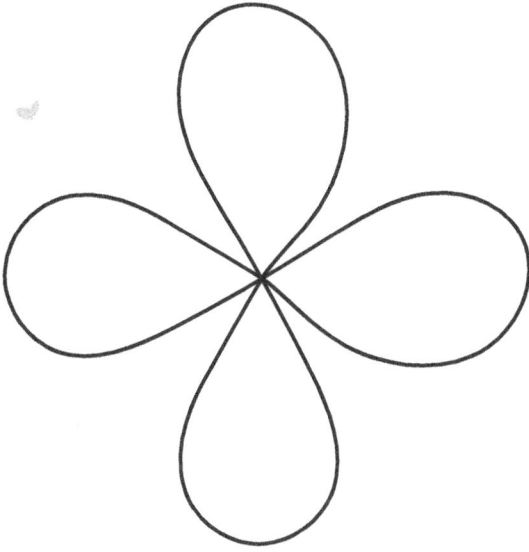

"Only you know what's hidden within yourself. It is your treasure that nobody can take away. It is you and no one else."

33rd message: LOVE - THE GUIDING PRINCIPLE WITH EVERYTHING YOU DO

Dear Sandra,

My medium, my angel, today's message is going to be short and sweet.

Whatever you are doing in your life, do it with love. Let this be your guiding stone. This book is written through my medium, Sandra — she is the bridge between us, your channel and mine. So, listen closely to her voice, for she has something meaningful to tell you today.

Your path is **life**. This life is inside your earthly form right here on this little Earth. You are given all of my support - take it when you want. You most often receive it in love. In my limitless, boundless love, in all of its beauty. Take it, do not push it away. Your life, interwoven with God's love, will raise you high where you'll fly like the angels, watching over and guarding you on your path. Every step is infused with our eternal watchfulness and then concluded in eternity. But before concluding it, give yourself a chance to make your walk on this earth infused with love. I cannot get past this without telling you, how much I love you and how much you are loved, my dear friends. You think that I have left you, that I have gone, but I tell you that I am always here. Here with you.

Your God.

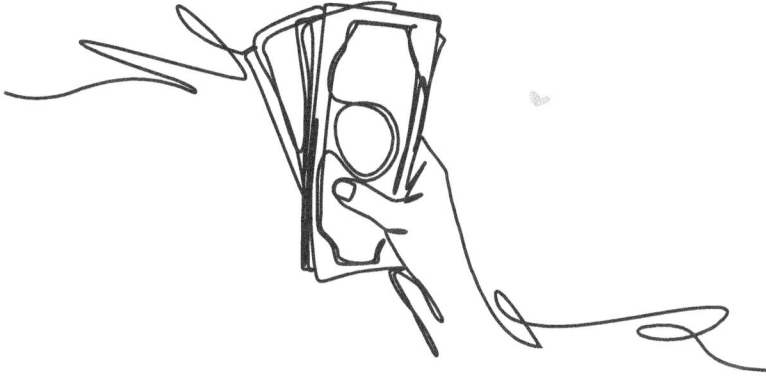

"Drive far around and you will see new cities and new places that will delight you. Leave your mark on them."

34th message: MANIFESTATION - SITTING IN A WHITE ROOM, INTO WHICH EVERYTHING FLOWS

Dear Sandra,

My angel, through your writing, I see the light of the world. Let your energy be beautiful, pure, and limitless. Come, let's now tell the world a new story. You'll write it down and I'll tell you.

The biggest sin in life is not being your own lord of the light of wealth born out of money. Money rules the world, they say. But what enables its acquisition is expressed in the images of coins, material things, and the eternally present sinful thought: "What and how to manifest everything we want?". Manifestation is nothing but easily obtaining money. Let this story about money be something beautiful and not something that will frustrate you and drive you to despair. You all wish for money, plenty. And let's say that you wish for 1000 dollars. What will you do to get them?

Will you go to the bank, rub your hands together, and earn them the honest way, or will you rather tell the universe: "Give me a thousand dollars!" Maybe one or both of them. Whichever one you choose, the biggest mistake you will most likely make later is grumbling to yourself that you don't have that money. But when the rabbit is stuck in the hole, when your head is filled with all the things you can't afford to buy, own, and have, is when you get that pain in your head, and so you yell to the sky.

Oh, how I would love to have some money, I need it, I don't have it...You say all of this. But have you maybe stopped to think that you can have it, that it simply comes to you, and you spend it? You don't have to jump for it, run to it, insinuate about it, get angry, or do push-ups to attract this money. You first ask for it nicely, and you feel yourself carrying it around like it's already on its way. You smell it, you see it, you carry it around in your bag, and you play with it in your safe.

You smell it and salivate over it, thinking how it's in your hands already, thinking it's yours. This feeling gives you "balls" to use a colloquial term, so you can then transition into the next feeling. And what will your next feeling be? Well, you're spending your money already, of course, and looking at things in the store, getting in the car you want to own, and then truly feeling and touching all of this and knowing inside yourself how you're already living with all the money that you want.

But will this money really come? It will if you act as if I just told you. But maybe it won't because you just won't be susceptible to it flying into your life. You won't feel the smell, the incredible feeling of spending and receiving this money, so it won't fly into your life when it could easily get right into your safe, bank account, or wallet by just flicking your finger and manifesting it there. That is when you'll say: "Darn, I don't have the money, I'm poor again, can't afford anything, the world is cruel and unfair to me, and most of the people are just trying to live day by day!" But what my friends have you done to invite it into your life?

Nothing. Absolutely nothing. You whined, cried, and yelled at the heavens and all those around because you're going crazy, not having enough to survive. But money is lying all around you. You just need to snap your finger – like you would a magic wand – and poof, it's there. But for some it is you'll say, for those rich ones and not for me, never for me. And why isn't it, my dear friends? Because **you don't let** it come into your beautiful life, because you live it like you do.

Now, believe! Believe that the 1000 dollars I was talking about at the beginning is rolling beneath your feet. Again, what do you do? Will you ask the sky, me, the universe, and your dearest loved ones up above to help you get that money? What will you do after that? Maybe wait again so there won't be anything. No financial shift. Yes, what will you do if you don't want there to be anything?

What you need to do is give yourself to the feeling, to feel the smell, the rustling of the paper, the feverish shopping theater of spending money in your thoughts, to be in your own little cloud so ready to receive this money that you can simply see it coming and making you happy. Making you happy to the point where you're happy that you received it. And the manifestation was successful.

You know, the manifestation is always successful, if we decide it and the following conditions are fulfilled. Let me list them:

- Prayer, the request, a look into the sky, and a soulful prayer intertwining the body and soul (deep prayer);

- A concrete amount you need to say, to tell the universe so it knows how much to deliver;

- The allowance for it all to come to you as it usually comes to people who want it.

The manifestation will happen when you are in a willing state, a state that will not rush you but will lead you to this money. And what is a state of allowance my darlings? It is like sitting in a white room filled with white light where everything radiates white. On top of the room is an opening through which everything flows with you sitting in the middle of this white light filled white room and you raise your head towards the opening and you say what you want. Then the sky directly to you, into your hands in a little pail delivers exactly what you wished for.

Let me draw it for you:

THE HEAVENS / THE UNIVERSE

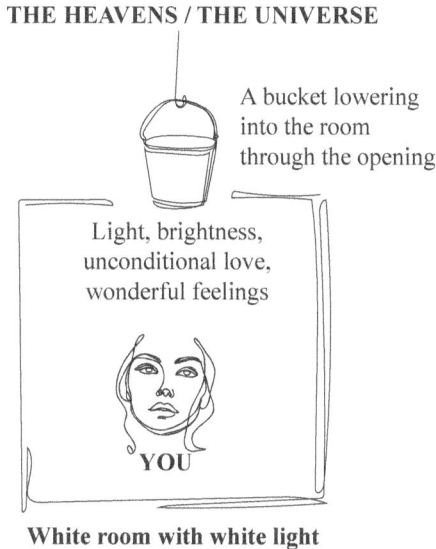

A bucket lowering into the room through the opening

Light, brightness, unconditional love, wonderful feelings

YOU

White room with white light

That is how it looks like my friends. Once you give in and trust, you live in pure limitless beauty of the heart and unconditional love, that is when the universe delivers to you everything you asked the sky. You don't need to do cartwheels, dig holes, or have bad thoughts because you don't have what you want, but just let it come to you. Rich people know this, and it's why money comes to them in greater and greater quantities. They let this happen, and they know that manifestation is a simple and very useful step to get to that money.

What makes a rich man different from a poor man? Only the mindset, faith, trust, feelings, and everything that leads to him allows him to get everything he wants.

Your God.

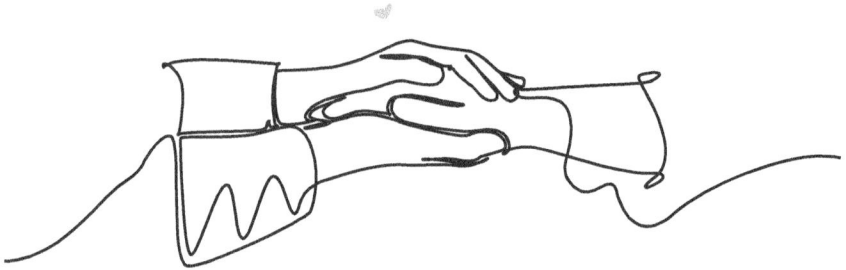

"Cultivate what you have, not what you want to have.
Gratitude is a beautiful look, don't lose it."

35th message: COMPASSION

We need to remember something, which belongs to the domain of the greatest qualities of man – **Compassion**. What is compassion? What do I want to tell you about it? Do you ever ask yourself, why is someone compassionate or dispassionate towards you? Do you ever ask yourself what is the one thing that makes you compassionate, forever friendly to the environment, to people, to animals?

That primacy within you, which never fades when someone throws themselves before your feed and looks at you with compassionate eyes and begs you to be nice to them, and you're good and you listen, return the smile and hug and move on... like someone, who hasn't forgotten to take with them the feeling of freely giving your compassion and bond to people, little children, animals, beautiful birds, the biggest stones on this world, to the turtle in the aquarium or to yourself.

Did the Millennium heart in the middle of the desert worry that it would not get water? Never. Because the compassionate act of someone brought water into the desert and poured it down the throat of the suffering, thirsty one. Three hundred tiny little *furballs* gathered to watch with admiration and great pride at this scene and *at the eyes and throat* of the one receiving this compassion. I cannot get through this without telling you why a compassionate creature cannot give their compassion when another needs it. It is because they do not carry it in their heart. They cannot carry it, because they cannot handle it. They cannot handle it in many forms. In a state of consciousness (when they are awake), when half asleep (when not so wakeful), and when they're sleeping (when not awake at all). That is where it all begins. Consciousness slowly creaks open the door to compassion and transforms it into an unfortunate action, unworthy of love. So, the heart is still half empty, because this feeling is still not there. But when the heart senses it, when out of the drowsiness or sleep comes that spark of sensing that prepares the human consciousness into the smallest step of consciously feeling some compassion, then the vibration moves. It moves in the right direction, and the heart senses the vibration and accepts it. So, compassion obtains its meaning of manifestation in a larger scope and pours out over everything. Over the eyes of the one sleeping when he is sad, loving when they are grumpy and in need of compassion, or merely the one who doesn't want anything and thinks that there is always something missing, including compassion, compassion for others, and himself.

You read that right – compassion for oneself. We can be compassionate to ourselves. Are you familiar with this? No, you're probably not. Can you tell me if you're very compassionate to others but not yourself? But why do you think like that when you must first be compassionate towards yourself. Compassionate to the part of yourself that protects you from the unfortunate acts stemming from the ego. The ego that steals your energy, that is the higher evil, that never rests and never lets you rest, even when you are calm and think you've won, it won't let you rest. It's then that it surprises you and shoots up to the surface. It's those times that compassion preaches to the ego, but the ego squeezes it, chokes it, and won't let it breathe. Simply say goodbye to the ego and build your own (capitalize it) NATURAL feeling of compassion.

Why did I say natural? Because it is always within you. This feeling has been naturally ingrained, but is always walked on, stomped on, trampled on, and silenced by the ego. In cases where you need to feel more compassion, the unnatural ego, write it "NOT YOURS", wakes up and chimes in, "Well, why should I have to be compassionate to someone or something, when they do not feel the same for me? Why should I give to others when they don't give to me?"

Ugh, we are so ego-driven. Just because old patterns and ways of thinking float up to the surface like excrement! So, we are moving forward to even more ego-driven actions until we feel no more compassion for anyone or anything.

So, let's take this one thing at a time. First, be aware of yourself, your beautiful, natural feeling of compassion, and compassion to yourself. Give this, do that. When you take this step, you can also throw yourself a little to the front and to the side, where you can give your compassion to someone else as well. Oh, how this will make you happy when that poor man, embraced with your compassion, livens up and thanks you for it. What else would he do but that when he gets from you a dose of beautiful compassion wrapped in the most beautiful feelings of joy? Well, he'll give you back his own wonderful feeling of compassion, and of course save some of you for himself. So here we are back at step one. Do you see how everything flows back and forth, from you to me and back again?

This is what we up here call LOVE. Once you give it – this time in the form of compassion – you also get it back. Isn't this it? Isn't this what we're looking for? Isn't this what we actually need? Don't be afraid of not getting it. First, find it within yourself and then pass it forward, and it will return to you like a boomerang.

Your God.

"Only focus your mind and thoughts on LOVE.
Limitless, unconditional LOVE.
It is the cure for everything."

36th message: WE ARE ONE. ALL IS ONE

Dear Sandra,

Dear light of the world, your voice reaches far into the millions of people. What is one voice that a person like you can share with the world, healing everyone against all the evil that is currently unraveling in this time and space you call Earth?

Our task is to spread this voice, the voice of love, because it is our message that should reach every home and every being on Earth. Today we're talking about Earth, our little Earth on which you people who are the most spiritual and are mostly spiritual beings live. Living in the environment of time and space. They are an illusion. It's illusory to imagine a time and space that doesn't exist. It is only a dimension that you currently inhabit. Life is inherent to every relationship that happens on this little Earth in time and space, while you're living every day of your earthly life.

You came here before your time to embody and live out a life story inside the mind that you inhabit every day on this beautiful little Earth. Perhaps you didn't imagine that you just flew here from some other different cosmos where time and space do not exist. Only souls live where you're from.

I cannot get past the fact that you do not realize that you are primarily a soul or spirit, whichever term you prefer. I call it a soul. The soul is your karma, your karmic record, your DNA that you've brought to this little Earth. It is written in the annals, written in your soul code, which only you can read during meditation on

Earth. When you are in a meditative state, your soul gets caught in a ritual, we call SOUL DRIVE. It's where the soul once again finds itself, looks for itself in the metaphysical state, and leaves this chaos and the chaotic dimension of earthly living you all love so much while staying on Earth. Your mind then is nothing, it does nothing, it doesn't think, it doesn't go forward or backward, it only rests and acts as if it were blind because it is resting in the complete darkness where it does not see, hear, or know anything.

So, my dear friends, what I wanted to tell you is that you can find your soul during meditation, during the meditation drive, and when the mind is silent, quiet, and dark. That is when the soul is home.

Home, from where it came. No, it is not at home on Earth but only a temporary resident who will soon leave. It will transform itself through the cloud, get to the other side, and only leave behind a coat of the body – the body coat.

When I talk about home, I'm not talking about the Earth, but our home up here for all of us in the soul part, where the souls have been living for millions and billions of years (the talk of time is for your sake, you seem to be used to it, my friends). Home lies only and solely in heaven. Within the divine kingdom of God (not the devil), faeries, angels, and all the heavenly beings.

Like in a fairy tale, you say. Well, this divine world of ours is a Fairy tale (with a capital F!), just like your Earth. You see, the difference is only in the fact that you've left thousands of lives in the kingdom of God, but only one on Earth. That is the biggest difference. Maybe you'll leave another one again sometime in another planetary space where you might embody next. Only your soul knows that.

When I talk about the Earth, I would like to give two warnings:

1. The worry about the poor little Earth, which you constantly exploit and don't take care of her at all.

2. The worry about the collective awareness that we are all ONE. That you are on Earth, everything and every single living being, all of nature, everything living and nonliving, all is ONE. Remember that well!

Why? Because we are ONE, we must worry that much more about the environment, nature, and the life-filled living on this little Earth. I'm not talking in wait when I wish you to consider everything as ONE. This means that your worry for the environment, the relationship between the environment and people, needs to stem from one equation:

We are ONE. All are ONE.

Because if we are all ONE, then it is impossible not to work out of love. If we are all ONE, then we must take care of nature, take care of the poor dying animals, love and respect each other boundlessly and infinitely. Can it really be like that? Too many times I notice how you treat your environment, how you pollute, how you treat your fellow people, how you treat the animals, how you don't love yourselves…

I look at all of that and wish to give you this message:

Be aware of your **ONE**ness and work in the name of **LOVE**. Your soul and your little Earth will be glad, and you will live the best embodied life. That is what I wanted to say.

Your God.

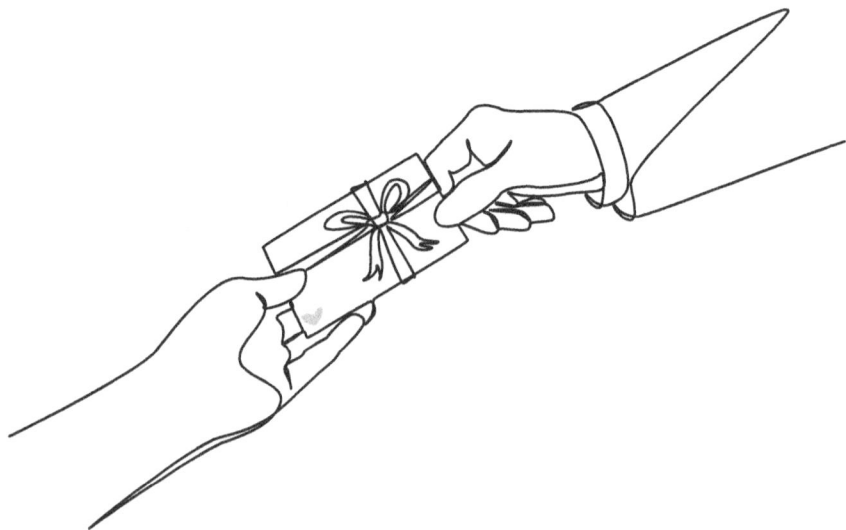

"While walking through the world, spread the seeds of love.
Do not be afraid of sowing many, many seeds.
They will grow and grow into something even greater."

37th message: GREED IS NOT A "PACKAGING" OF LOVE

Being greedy is a small thing. Not the greatest virtue, but a small thing that doesn't lead towards divinity. It does not lead to a fulfilled life.

Greed is not necessary. It is not your virtue; it does not originate from the divine but from the ego. It is the eternal desire to be the best, the biggest, the richest, the greatest, and so make you feel bigger, richer, greater, and in the end, falsely happy. But are you really? No, never! It is an addiction, my friends.

The desire for a bigger home so you can justify your existence by proving your wealthy status does not make you beautiful or happy. This black addiction is the reflection of your ego, the ego of a person driven by greed and, in the end, suffocated by it.

This emotion of the ego, when it manipulates the mind for something that exploits another person, demands too high a cost, which in the end is always paid by the person and their human mind. Be it more money, a mindset of domination, or something else, it is not your job to make it happen.

This only drags you further into the pit of despair. A bottomless pit that in the end sucks you down into a world of misery, ugliness, dispassion, and everything opposite to light, to love. Because in the end, believe me, you remain alone, alone with your greedy ways. Because in the end, these actions have nothing in common with your DNA of the soul, the DNA that cannot write down these actions into itself. This is not in a soul's DNA because the revelation of the soul never hinges on actions such as these, much less greed in the sense of the actions of the soul upon the ego. This is simply not its DNA. Never was and never will be. Why? Because it is not divinity, it is not a "package" of love but of ego, which has nothing to do with divinity.

Every person deserves everything in this world, but because of greed never achieve it. Greed is not a poem of the soul but a song of the ego. Not a song sung by the soul but one by the ego. So remember, always when you feel the lust of egoistic greed, stop yourself and simply turn toward the light, which will bring you to divinity.

Your God.

"Be optimistic, life will pay it back. All of it."

38th message: STORY OF THE WALLET - WHEN THE FORCES OF EGO ARE STRONGER THAN LOVE

Dear Sandra,

My angel, let only love guide you every day. When I speak with you, I wish that you would take my words into the world among the people who will read them and be healed by them. The most beautiful feeling is that I can again deliver my message. A personal message just from me. From the heavenly kingdom filled with angels, divine beings, and beings of light who shine upon your little Earth. How many times do you perchance look at the sky and say:

"O God, give me this and give me that, come on, God help me, God, oh God, how I'm unhappy and you're not helping me! O, my angels, where are you when I need you the most?"

You yell these words into the sky, looking with begging eyes and hands, and wondering whether I am even here and whether I even exist. Of course, I am here. Of course, I exist. I am always here. Even inside your divine body, when you're not deceiving yourself, and chasing me away into far-off lands, you call other dimensions by your egoism.

I am not in other dimensions. I, God, am always here, present inside of you. How were you born? How do you think that you incarnated into your divine body? Through your mother, yes, however, this is just a transformation from a heavenly soul body from the other side, the side of the divine, however, you wish to call it, through the uterus into the body of your mother and into this wonderful world. Let this make you think that I have always been and always will be present inside of you, inside your soul, inside your body-soul balance, which you sometimes destroy.

The story is always finished when you break the soul-body peace. Your thoughtfulness wants something that hasn't grown from love and wishes to manifest it through actions that are not love. That is when I'm not inside of you. That's when you move away from me when your soul no longer wishes for my compassion, my loving sparks that created you. Your feelings then become internal unrest, fear, despair, and everything is not connected to me.

So please understand that the messages I'm giving to you when you ask for them are not just a superficial ballad or a hymn to quickly sing away, but my leadership to you personally. To your soul, your higher self, who isn't tuned quite right, asking for my beautiful guidance that brings you to the right path you dreamt about when you came here and incarnated.

Do you think that you're alone, my dear friends, that you were abandoned by God, as you like to say? No, you were not! I am always here with you except when you move away from me. If you do not, I wish to come closer to your request. But only your request, because I do not intervene directly except if it's an emergency, or you would be in danger, or pushed towards death. That is when I intervene with my divine leadership and with my divine voice, which you can hear or not. To hear it or not is your decision, and as you decide to hear it and get ready to listen and recognize me again on the path, you can catch me. What's been given to you since birth is this divine love being forged within you, my friends. Only you can take it away. Even the angels are always present and by your side.

Just call them when you need them and ask them for help. One is always on your left shoulder, sitting and breathing behind your neck. Waiting and waiting when Sandra or the 7 billion incarnated people will ask and call for help, when their wagon gets detached from the train and possibly derails off the tracks far away somewhere.

That is when your guardian angel steps in to help and sends you beautiful lyrics through music, or a message through a license plate you see, or on a shirt, perhaps you find a coin or other object. This is an angel giving you a warning and showing you the way forward. But the angels won't solve the situations instead of you and make decisions for you. Never! That will never happen!

They only show you the path, the magical path that sends you on the right track to your train. Remember the story of the train and little wagons? This is that story.

There was a lady who asked me for help before because she lost her wallet filled with her documents and money. I heard her wish right away. She was very impatient and reluctant, and she wished for my intervention immediately.

You know, I hear every request right away, and I hear hers too, but her low vibration, disagreeableness, and her anger about not finding the wallet cost her a lot of her nerves. Her unrecognizable deception hypnotized face, declaring that God doesn't exist anyway – those were her words – portrayed the disapproval of all forces that were at work trying to find her wallet quickly.

The forces couldn't function because her ego was defeating the efforts of the angels and me, God, trying to find this wallet and quickly return it to this lady.

She became even more impatient and hopeless, and without faith, the forces of the ego were overcoming the mighty forces of the universe, which are settling the final steps in finding and solving her situation with the wallet. We couldn't harmonize her lack of faith and trust in the force, this mighty divine force that orders everything on this planet, the cosmos, and every dimension.

Look now how this worked:

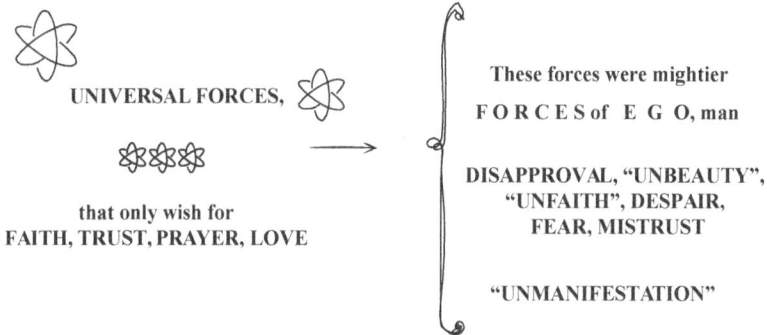

UNIVERSAL FORCES,

that only wish for
FAITH, TRUST, PRAYER, LOVE

These forces were mightier
F O R C E S of E G O, man

DISAPPROVAL, "UNBEAUTY",
"UNFAITH", DESPAIR,
FEAR, MISTRUST

"UNMANIFESTATION"

So, the lady is without her wallet to this day. Do you think she's sorry? Yes. Today she's already sorry about it, feels guilty about it, and is making herself into the biggest victim in the world for losing all her documents and money that's being spent by another right now (there were several hundred dollar bills in the wallet), and because some misfit took all her documents and ripped them or used them for some other purposes and then spent all of the money.

The lady is now angry at the authorities who couldn't help, is angry at the incompetent officials who didn't know how to help and is playing the role of the miserable victim of thievery. The story is real and sounds quite rigid, doesn't it?

The forces have done their part. If she had only let herself give in and begin to trust, if she had let go of her insecurity and not gotten angry, the forces of love could have, but a moment later, brought her wallet right back to her.

The lady lost her wallet around the corner, and it was found by a 13-year-old. What do you think he did with it? He bought the bike he wanted after all that time. He left the documents in the shaft that no one was ever going to open. So that's the story that can happen to you, and believe me happens quite often to countless numbers of people.

Be with love, my friends,

Your God.

"You will receive what you think, the right one
and the wrong one."

39th message: SICKNESS IS A SIGN OF THE ABSENCE OF LOVE

Dear Sandra,

My angel, I love you immeasurably, so much so that I could give my life for you. Still, my life I cannot give because I am undying, I am eternal. But I can guide you and be within you when you wish for me to be. The gift of your hearing me and writing this down is boundless and eternal. Your ability to hear me is binding both for you and those who are going to read this and will be healed with every word of mine, because I, God, am a healer. I heal you; I beat inside of you like health. When you do not move away from me, you are healthy. Did you know, my dear friends, that sickness is nothing but your absence, distance, and flight from me, from the divine energy that is always within you, that flows throughout your body like blood when you are within the love, the light, my light? My dear children, children of the Creator and the light, in you there exists nothing else but divinity, divine energy, which you reject when you distance yourself. Your sickness is shown in a thousand and one diseases that are pestering you. This is the absence of health, **sickness is the absence of health; sickness is the absence of love**.

The simple equation:

ILLNESS = ABSENCE OF HEALTH = ABSENCE OF LOVE

So, what to do when you are unhealthy? When are you sick? Go, connect again with me, turn on the light inside yourself, bring your divinity back into your body and mind, and there, there you will be in a state of divinity and love. If you are pestered by different disorders, dependencies, and all unhealthy things inside of you, then you are not in a state of love. That is when you don't love yourself but are combating your fears, frights, and ugly situations, then your heart is not open and does not beat in the rhythm of love. Filled with hatred, piles of rudeness, and "deadly Viking games" that lead you nowhere and pester you hour after hour and weaken your mind and body. Then it's time for your famous "Doctor" who prescribes medicine for your situation. Then you succumb to another addiction that has no end in sight. You're falling into repeated pain because of n e u r o t i c s i t u a t i o n s a n d d e p r e s s i v e d i s o r d e r s of neo-healing, and the circle is complete. It doesn't let you leave.

Doesn't ever let you leave.

So my dear friends, choose love because your healing energy flows through you and heals you.

That's when you can achieve everything. Absolutely everything. Including your health. You are not sick because you allow health to seep through and flow through you.

Your channels are clean, fluid, and fluent because the Love in your cells works in a way that makes them healthy and clean and keeps the chakras flowing.

Your energy just glows from the flow of energy from your head to your feet and back again. That, my dear friends, is when you work and are in a state of love. When you are in a state of healing, good feeling, beautiful, everything is beautiful.

That is when you don't get sick. That is when you are reliving health in all its forms: the mind, the body, and the spirit. So, I say to your soul and heart, **become only love, the equal sign to your health**.

Your God.

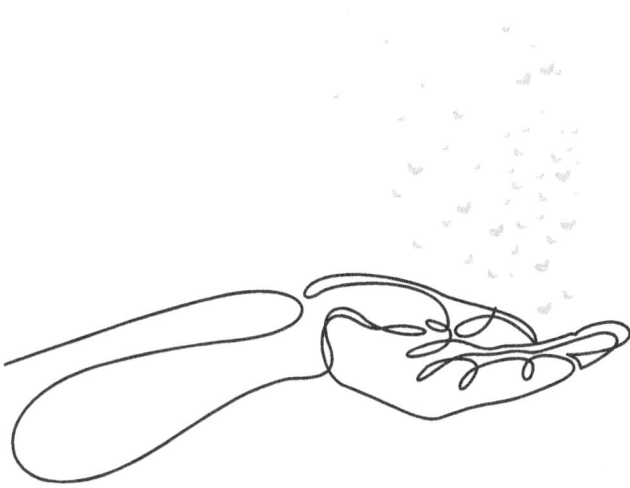

"The head should be open to beautiful things. You don't need clutter in there anyway. "

40th message: DON'T PRETEND TO BE POOR

Dear Sandra,

My angel, let your hand take my message into the world. Let me tell you something about miserliness and penny-pinching. That is nothing more than acting out of a lack of self-confidence, lack of plenty, and lack of love.

When you squeeze money in your fist, you are not doing yourself any favor! You constantly act as if something is missing, that you are in need. But there is plenty enough for everyone. I give every single one everything, in any form they want, even money. There is as much of that in the world as you wish, available to everyone should they just want it. So don't close your fist to which you can't put the money you don't have. This is not Godly, it doesn't come from divine energy. When you are lacking, you are not acting out of love. What I told you about health also applies to stinginess, non-possession, and a life of lack. This is a deficit that doesn't come from your love.

Why must you save so much when you can have as much money as you want every moment of every day? Do you go to the store to get food every day? Do you eat every day? So, this is the same. This is the same as if you must eat every day. If you want a hundred, a thousand, or I don't know how many dollars, go and take it the same way you do when you go to the store.

Why do you think there is no money for you? Why do you think that way, my dear friends? Why do you squeeze the empty fist and feel as if you don't have it? That is nothing but a lack of love. You are not worthy of this feeling. This is not a feeling that comes from you but from your lower self. The lower self again succumbs to the ego, which is killing it with a stick, prodding it to drown you in the water that is dragging you into the depths.

Don't let yourself be fooled, dear friends, there is enough money for everyone. Abandon the temptations of saving for yourself, others, and the world because you think that you don't have enough and that you are not worth it, that you can't get what you want, and are being driven into even more despair because of it. Misery and poverty are a state of your spirit, which leads you into even greater misery. Why do you think that, compared to others, you are not worthy of receiving money, and so instead you act poor?

Yes, you heard me right, I said you are acting poor. You are **acting poor**, acting as someone who lacks. How can someone be poor and without money when he is in this world of plenty with money in all its forms on this little Earth? My dear friend, it's because YOU ARE ACTING POOR!

Everything only originates from you, from your mindset, be it the mindset you gained in your childhood or the mindset you gained on your journey of life.

I don't have, I don't want, I can't = **WEAKNESS**
 POVERTY
 LACK OF ABUNDANCE
 LACK OF LOVE
 LACK OF DIVINITY
 EGO

So I'm telling you, my dear friend, be open, open your heart, it's not that hard! Is it really that hard? It's not! Just act differently. Look inside yourself, get in closer, internalize your power and love, and your days will be filled with love, which will bring into your life every dollar you will ever need.

Let life come to you, act in such a way that life will keep coming to you in all its forms, even in the form of money, and so turn on the light inside of you!

Your God.

"Be beautiful forever, beauty is the key."

41st message: ONE DAY BE UNCONDITIONAL LOVE

Dear Sandra,

My angel, writing this book, I bless you with the pure, boundless, pure, and beautiful love as radiant as the water in a well.

You are my assistant, my messenger bringing this message to all the bodies on this little Earth. Our little Earth is round, and on it live a billion incarnated beings, created by the Creator, created by God, who every day walk, dance, move, think, sunbathe, and make the Earth more beautiful.

Their bodies are unique, everyone is different from everyone else. However, their soul only belongs to one single soul, divine energy. The soul is eternal, ever-present, God-given, immortal, and beautiful. Still, it happens that a body will get sick and tired, that it will not think nice thoughts and make human mistakes which cost it its eternal peace, so I would like to say how important it is that you love each other, that you love others, and that you **cultivate beautiful relations**.

Relations filled with life will contribute to the planet and make sure that the soul is forever growing and developing. Your bodies are the indicator of your relationships. Your relationship to yourself, fellow man, and others, be it animal, stone, or any other person. I am forever interested in your relationships with everyone and everything.

Whether you intend to channel your energy into a good or bad relationship is guided by your mindset. When I'm talking to you about your relationships, I'm again thinking about love. The love you give and the love you receive, or don't receive. The love you hold back and the love you don't receive. It is like a boomerang.

RELATIONSHIPS   ↔   RELATIONSHIPS

What do you give? What do you get? Look!

The story is simple. It flows from up here, from me.

Oh, this God, you'll say, what a jester! But this is the sole and only truth – to be connected with the bearded elderly gentleman up above. Not at all. Not an old man. He is not old. He doesn't have a gray old beard. He's not dressed. He is not mortal. He is just energy. The old man you see in your eyes, on the TV screen as he has been so often portrayed to you, is pure immortal, all-encompassing, eternal, forever living, beautiful light energy.

When you let it into your body, your mindful body, you don't even need to let it in because it's been there all along, you simply mustn't move away from it. When you move away, you must let it back in again by taking it back and plugging yourself into it.

Then my dear friends, everything puts itself back into order. Then you're connected, as they say, to me. The invisible radiance, light, with divine energy, transports you into the most beautiful relationships in this world. And those relationships then last as long as you're connected. Oh, how beautiful it is to get a flower from someone whom you love, respect, cherish, and who loves you back, too.

When this happens, you don't ask yourself what if, should I, what will be, why wasn't there, because it wasn't, because it won't, will it not... Then you're simply living, here and now on this beautiful little Earth, on this planet in this spatial and temporal dimension, which is actually "up" here with me, my dear friends, especially the mind... Only me, my angels, and all the other divine beings.

Your relationships, good and bad, from day to day, will be the way you want, and let them be. Be the **unconditional love** for one day, try it, my dear friends, to be loved unconditionally for just one little day. What do you think your relationships with yourself and the other people and living beings around you will be like?

Want me to tell you?

BEAUTIFUL. DIVINE. GOD GIVEN. LIVING!

What do you think unconditional love in a relationship is? Something more beautiful than can ever happen to you, like the birth of a child. It's the magical feeling that infuses you with boundless giving love. It is the state of spirit that is exclusively NATURAL. Use big letters because that's what the spirit is, truthfully like. Just like that, and nothing else in the light of unconditional love, and that's that.

That is when you are transported to the greatest heights of relationships, to the highest vibrational peaks, where you feel as if you are in the clouds of joy, happiness, understanding, harmony, and all the beautiful things accompanying you in relationships, prompting you to stay. And do you know why? Because when you're there, you come home. That is your true self, your home.

So, I tell you, allow yourself just one day when you gift yourself the opportunity to experience being in relationships as true, unconditional love. Love that only gives and expects nothing in return, love that doesn't judge and accepts everything for what it is, and demands nothing in return. It just is, here and now. Here in the grand style a forever-loving soul, filled with joy and happiness. Then call me and let me know, my dear friends, if it's worth it to be unconditionally loving and to give unconditional love.

When you feel and sense this powerful beauty in relationships for just one day, trust me, you will want more and more, one more day, two more days, and more and more until you become unconditional love. Then your vibration will be so high that it will spread the vibration of your soul into the skies, to me.

You'll strengthen your love in your relationships and actions; you'll be spreading it to others, and the collective consciousness will be raised everywhere. This little Earth will then be even more beautiful and exist on higher energy. That is what I'm waiting for. That is what I expect from you, my dear friends, so I call on you – have and **be** in your relationships for at least a day of beautiful, **unconditional love!**

Your God.

"Your heart is like a muscled body. The more you fill it with love,
the more muscled and suffused with love, it will become."

42nd message: THE RITUAL OF UNCONDITIONAL LOVE

Dear Sandra,

My angel, to love is the greatest gift that a person can taste in their human life on this little Earth.

Is there anything more beautiful than knowing how to love? Write, dear Sandra the word "Love" with a capital letter because it deserves it. When you are loved, when you know and wish to love (yourself and others), you always make sure that it's all going in the right direction.

Nothing can ever overcome you, nothing can change you, nothing can turn you away from the true path you wish to walk, and you were meant to walk. It depends on you what you do in the moment of insincerity, lack of plenty, and misfortune, because then you are not in a state when you love and are loved. Your misfortune and lack of plenty are indicators of your mindful and mental poverty, which is not in line with you or your wishes. Synchronicity can be achieved with love for yourself and others.

Do you see how often I repeat this? Of course, this will be the book of love, a book that talks and informs that love is the only guidance for all things that are relevant to man. But how do you recognize love?

Easy. It is grace, the happy component wrapped in harmony, beauty, a shine of everyday action, and wanting in all directions and areas of life. You cannot miss it if you do the work of love. It is the one tool for a happy, harmonious life full of plenty. When you are not in a state to give and receive love, you are not on the wavelength or waves of divinity. That is when you are not living your divinity, and that is what I've been telling you all along.

Be loving, good, happy, beautiful, and compassionate, be as open as you can be with an open heart, stare into the sky and the world, because the open heart is subservient to the greatest happiness. When a person opens their heart, he is like an open book, which you still need to read. Read it in the style of a beautiful romance and not an ugly crime novel. I, God, am not here to lecture you but to help you.

But what will you do, my little ones, when the arrow of love misses you, when it flies past you and does not take you into the mindful part of self and being, and will not let you breathe? That is when you grab your head, shake it very, very hard, and say:

"Let all wrong and misshapen things that do not come from my love leave my head, body, and mind now!"

Then spin three times, shaking your head, shaking your arms and legs, and feeling the negativity released into a cloud, a cloud which you then send into the light! Do this in the morning when you get up, and you can do it throughout the day, and do it before you go to sleep. Do it, it's liberating! It will liberate you from all binds that bind you and don't originate from love. Then you feel how, within you, from the Godly heavens through the top of your head comes light, shining, beautiful, white, gracious, and divine.

This is the divine energy that you allow to run through your body and mind, like blood through a vein. In each corner of your body, you feel it and imagine that within you exists only unconditional love. Do this. I call this the ritual of love. The ritual of UNCONDITIONAL LOVE.

And life will be easier, your fears and everything that does not belong within you will dissipate. The more you do this, the "healthier" you will become and the more in touch with me and your divinity you will be. Then you will not have a care in the world anymore, and you will not live in fear, and you will not have ugly relationships or be without money. Your happiness, harmony, comfort, and plenty will take the main stage in your life. Do not forsake this, my dear friends, do not forsake the permission to live divinity, it is priceless!

I tell you, be grateful for all you have in life; an allowance is worth its weight in gold. I will tell you about my gratitude another time.

Sandra, my dear angel, will remind me of this topic again in the future, won't you, Sandra?

Now, live your divinity!

Your God.

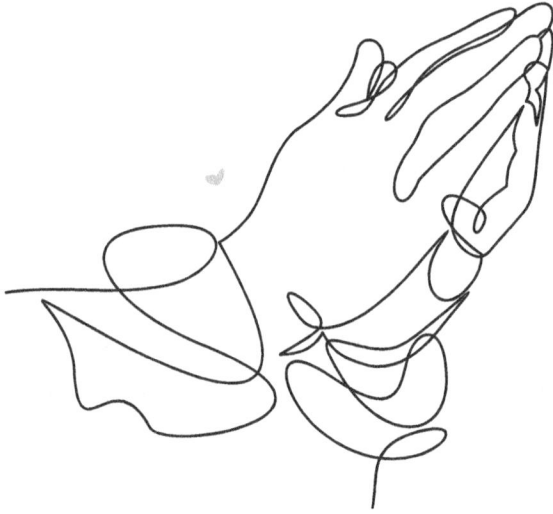

"Look at your things and only meddle in those of others when they ask you to."

2nd October 2019

43rd message: GRATITUDE AND THE COLLECTIVE HEART

My dear angel Sandra,

Today, we are going to touch on gratitude! Thank you for reminding me of this beautiful thing (I reminded him of it before I connected with him), this wonderful remembering, which everyone should know and feel when they go through every single day.

What do I wish to tell you, my dear friends, about gratitude? That you should practice it every day, the same as love, because it is the highest point of love, it is the highest point of vibration when we are near the point of love.

LOVE $\rightarrow$ **is the highest vibration**

(divine energy with the highest vibration)

then

G R A T I T U D E #

(gets very near the point of love, where the soul vibrates)

I hope you understand me: The highest point of vibration, the highest vibration in the divine sense, is love. Like this:

LOVE

G R A T I T U D E #
Aligned with the higest vibration point,
that is love. It's when we are happy,
harmonious, beautiful, and we vibrate in love.

Fear, negativity, disrespect, despair,
lack of self confidence, "unbeauty",
bad relationships.

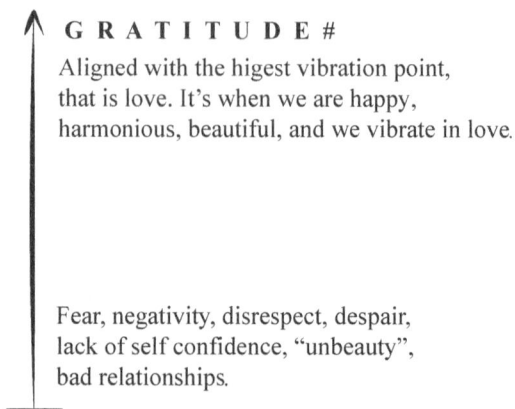

I showed it to you, so it's easier for you to imagine. But I must tell you that gratitude is not something you need to practice every day; gratitude is something you need to live with.

To live and be grateful is such a beautiful feeling that I don't know why every single person today doesn't feel gratitude when it is so natural and intoxicating to be grateful. When you are grateful, you are immeasurably happy, joyous, and everything looks beautiful as you look at the world in a different light – a sunny, beautiful light.

But I need to say that you need to know how to feel it. To be grateful is itself a small bit of gratitude on its own. Besides you being alone at the time, nothing can escape your grasp. When you feel gratitude, everything on Earth positions itself on the right side and is driving you towards your mission on this little Earth. Every morning when you get up, take a stretch, and then think and FEEL everything you can be grateful for immediately when you put on your morning slippers and robe. Many things. Countless things, and if you're not a morning type person, try to start with at least 5 things that can wake up the sun of gratitude.

And when you say these wishes and the mantra of gratitude, try to keep this feeling in your heart, and from your first grateful breath let your heart become so wide and open that it will take you into the skies.

Like this: **HEART** of a person

HEART of a person

That is how your heart opens up in the morning, but when you start your day with gratitude, then it goes like this: **COLLECTIVE** heart

COLLECTIVE heart

You see when you are grateful for the shower, the healthy cat, your fingers on your legs, your awesome mattress on which you've gotten the best night's sleep, the heart in the body, your physical heart is getting a greater and wider shape, expanding from minute to minute and you can FEEL IT (don't just think and say the thoughts of gratitude!). Your heart is becoming like a pump. Isn't this beautiful? It is! Why? Because then you are the highest point of vibration, you are vibrating in the style of love.

This vibration doesn't just reach you, but you are transmitting it into the world, to the collective life on this little Earth. When you are with your coffee in your hand, ready in your spirit of gratitude, and are leaving for work, you are full of contagious energy because you are vibrating with love.

When you're going to work and you arrive at the door of your office vibrating like this with an open heart, your energy just wafts around and attracts others with similarly open hearts. And the more grateful you are, the more your heart is pumped up, the more open you are, the more and more of those with a pumped-up vibrating heart become stuck to you.

COLLECTIVE love

a person

This is how big the collective heart looks when it is multiplied by a countless number of other gratitude-fueled hearts. It is a large collective heart.

COLLECTIVE heart

The Earth is opening up, the collective heart will keep

becoming bigger because more and more people are grateful for all sorts of things! But some are never grateful for anything, and those who will begin to fall off the collective heart and start falling into the depths.

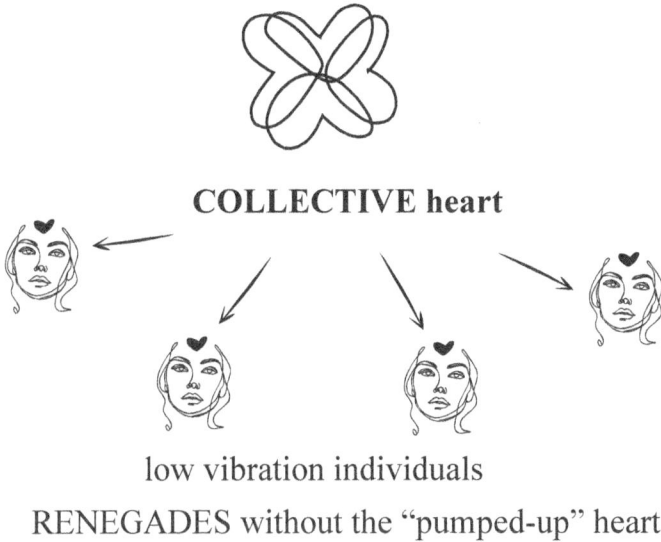

COLLECTIVE heart

low vibration individuals
RENEGADES without the "pumped-up" heart

What I wish to tell you is to hold to the collective heart and be a little bit grateful every day, and then every day a little bit more. And the collective heart will grow from day to day, and the Earth will wake up in a new consciousness. It is the only chance for it to survive, otherwise, it won't. So be part of the great collective heart!

Your God.

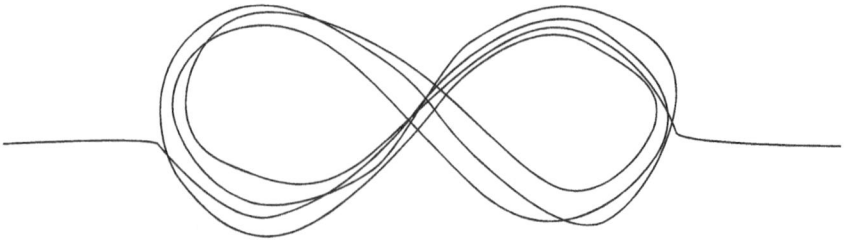

"You are not here to cry and grieve.
You are here only to give love."

44th message: DEATH DOES NOT EXIST; THE SOUL IS ETERNAL

Dear Sandra,

My angel, take my message of today to all the people on this Earth. How many times must I tell you that love is the light of this world? I wish for the awareness in people that this is the only true path, to be drenched in love. Love for yourself and love for others, love for living beings, and love for all material and immaterial things.

Your spirit is always here and watches over you. It's not hiding. There is nothing anywhere for you in your spirit without love. Let me tell you that all your actions affect everything. Absolutely everything.

This little Earth and its vibrations. Because we are all one. We are all ONE. It's not about money, greed, or something material, it's about that feeling of floating in the empty mass like in a bubble. That feeling is the one that takes you to the other side, the side where your eye does not have access, where your fingers do not feel, and your senses do not smell or sense. That is where your home is, your beautiful home. Heads there have no spirit of time; everything is empty, limitless, and infinite.

I'm telling you because that is where you come from, and that is where you're going with your soul. To a better world, more beautiful than you can imagine. Your soulfulness and your mindful restlessness are something you need to remove, so it's good that you recognize it and throw it away. It doesn't agree with you. You need to leave the deepest surfaces of this world to see the shine on the other side. It's not about a material shine but a pure spiritual shine. The shine you'll see when you get here. This is where I am home, and my home is always here. This is your home too, except you're spending a little time on this little Earth, in your body and your mind. You will overcome all that and return. Do not fear the passage, for it is the most natural thing that can happen to you.

It's the beauty that I cannot describe. You forever stay here in this light, this magical world you see, and will have forever. Here you don't need money, fur coats, or beautiful lipsticks; here you just are. You just are as if you are a bird on a branch, sitting on a transformer, looking up into the sky. It just is. Look, you're not all receptive to this kind of thinking, there are not a lot of you who think like this, as your mentality doesn't allow you to. You go into other, more material spheres. It's where your ego feels more at home. That is, for the most part, more like home to you, so I want you to listen now when I tell you that this is the time for you to think it over and imagine your existence here on this little Earth is not eternal, and that you come home to me. So don't be afraid to return. Your return will be blessed, you'll see. I will take care of it, so don't be afraid!

Do you sometimes think about returning? Oh yes, some of you think about returning — some of you YES, but most of you, NO! Why not? Because your life here in this material universe is so beautiful, right? You see everything, you hear everything, you feel, you put on your shoes and smile and look in the mirror, you have money, or you don't, and everything is running along in reality, in the material spirit, and you say: "Oh, why should I go back there? I'm only here on earth for a short time. NO, I'm not going!" You all scream: "No, I'm not going back there!"

Have you ever thought that it's good here, that you are actually home? No, you haven't! You see, my friends, you need to examine that head of yours a little more and feel yourself in your new home. Here you don't need anything, everything here is beautiful, and how it's supposed to be. When your "time" comes, even though time doesn't exist, you will be here. It's then that you will take off your body coat and leave it there on Earth, and your spirit will come back here from whence you've come.

You will come home, and your soul will be home again. Putting off your coat will be a one-time thing, invisible, so easy that you won't even know you're already home, with me. You will be so joyous upon your arrival into this homeliness, so I'm telling you, you will never wish to go back to this little Earth. The glamor and beauty of Earth will not tempt you again because this home is brighter, more beautiful, shining, and eternal. That will be the story you will write down. Your breakthrough from the unknown to the known, am I right? That little bit of what you know will remain for you to carry forward when you go home and are there forever with me at the highest possible vibration.

Do not think bad thoughts about needing to die right now. I'm not talking about that; I'm talking about the passage from your body and your return home. I'm expecting you here as a mother awaits the return of her child. Do not fear death, my little ones, that is my message for today, because death does not exist, and your soul is eternal. It only returns home where I'm waiting for it, and where it's beautiful. So, my dear friends, death is a beautiful event that leads you into eternal paradise. Not the **paradise** on earth, but the one in divinity.

Your God.

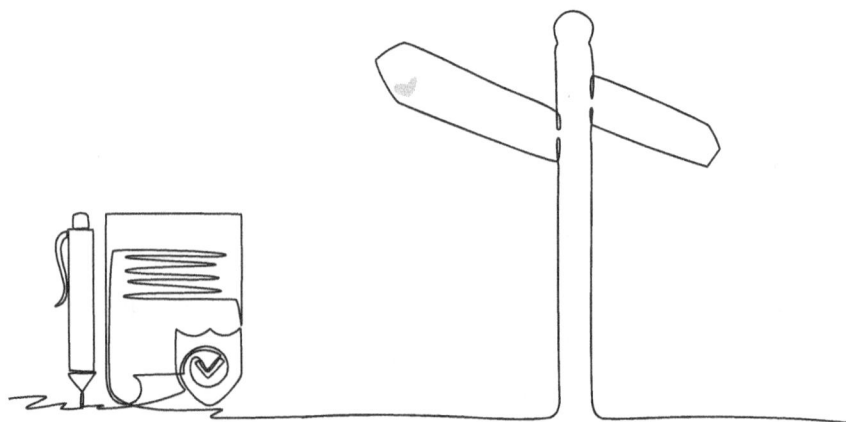

"The shackles and chains you don, are a message from
your head, your mind."

45th message: THE SOUL CONTRACT AND THE SIGNPOSTS OF LIFE

Dear Sandra,

My angel, there is so much you need to tell the world with this book to the people who are already waiting in the world for my messages to reach them.

Let it be the will of the people who read this book to be open to receiving my messages, because the messages I give you, my dear friends, are life. Life here and now on this little Earth. Do not shield your eyes from the fact that I am here, here forever now and everywhere you are. Because you were born from me, God.

Now let's go in order here. Your life here is your own, and let it be as beautiful as possible. What we've written down on paper in the **contract** before you've come to this dimension and this body has already been determined. That is your mission on this little Earth. You cannot change it, but you can enjoy it if you want to, and know-how. This is not a contract that can be notarized, but it is a sort of guideline for what awaits your soul on the planet while you're living. It is written, and agreed upon, and nothing can be changed. But you can, my dear, change the direction of the path by how you think. Do you think out of love or not? Based on whether your actions are out of love or not depends on where and, most of all, **how** you get where you're going. Where are you going? Where you're going is determined in the soul contract composed together by the souls themselves before you've embodied into this beautiful life experience. And if I tell you now that this contract is by my side all the time and I guard it diligently for every single individual in a safe, you're going to laugh.

Hahaha, how can God have a contract. How did he create it for us?... Haha, and how does he keep it? In a safe? This is all make-believe, you'll say, my dear friends.

Oh no, not at all! I'm telling you, now take a breath and believe my dear friends. What and who you will be, where you are going to go and with who you'll have children, who your mother and father are going to be, what your mission in life is going to be, all of this, my dear human, is written down and set in this spiritual world where everything is written down and determined in a kind of – using an earthly term – contract. In it, up here, in this divine kingdom, even before we sent you down to Earth with a spark of divinity, light, and love through your mother's womb and ignited a spark in you, we wrote everything down beautifully. I want to show you an example of the contract we souls make for each individual, which is embodied on this little Earth:

Write this down:

Soul contract for Angela:

- Parents: Ivana and Rafael
- Partners: Mathew
- Job: healthcare
- Profession: doctor, writer (higher education)
- Kids: Paulina and Matteo
- Grandsons: Emanuel, Jacob, and Gabriela

- Life's mission: The life mission of Angela, our angel, which we have embodied on the earth, is to spread love. To spread love to all the people and all the living beings. Angela is our angel, who has an enormous power to heal and can heal any soul and every living being. Our angel Angela has her divine soul twin (twin flame). It is the man who is her partner. Among twenty-five thousand twin souls that incarnate on Earth, we have found Angela's twin flame—one that is also very great, which is an extraordinary rarity, as a twin soul incarnates on Earth, as already mentioned, in only twenty-five thousand cases.

Angela's mission is to first write a book, take it into the world, and use it to heal people. But first, she must heal her twin soul. While healing her, she heals herself. But what is healing that our angel Angela is performing? It's the act of giving love. Angela is unconditional love. She must spread this love throughout the world. That is her mission, her calling: to bring awareness to people, to elevate them to a higher vibration, so this small Earth can rise to a higher vibration, and so that people begin to think like our angel, Angela, in the light of love. The love of one person can influence ten people multiplicatively.

What the contract states is a determined path, but how you intend to realize that path and your mission is up to you. That is left up to you. If you are sent to this earth so that you become a top-level athlete, but you do not fulfill your mission through steps filled with love, then you will hardly become an incredible athlete. Do you understand me? You cannot become something if it did not grow out of a quality seed. What I want to tell you is that the direction and way you decide to complete your mission lie within you and are dependent on you. The signposts are yours; they are not specified in the contract. The main ingredients, like in a soup, are already determined, and we already know the spices, but how the soup will finally smell and what becomes of it is up to the chef and the ingredients he will throw into it.

I'm sure that my guidance nicely affects which way the signpost is turned. Left, right, straight, wherever you say. Someone can tell you to go left, but if you decide to go right, that is your decision. This depends on the basis you accept it from. When you operate out of love, I can assure you that all of your choices are correct and are leading you in the right direction. But when you don't operate out of love, you are going in a direction that will not be optimal for you.

As you see, the guidepost is always love. It's what I've been telling you the whole time. I'm like a broken record. But love is a thread, it is the connecting link that connects everything. Connect everything front and back. You must only operate out of love, and everything will be good. Everything will work out in line with the contract in the way that is best for you. Never despair and say: "Oh, this love again; God is always bothering me with it ..." No, it truly is the guidepost of everything.

So, now work in line with the clauses of your contract in the spirit of love, my friends.

Your God.

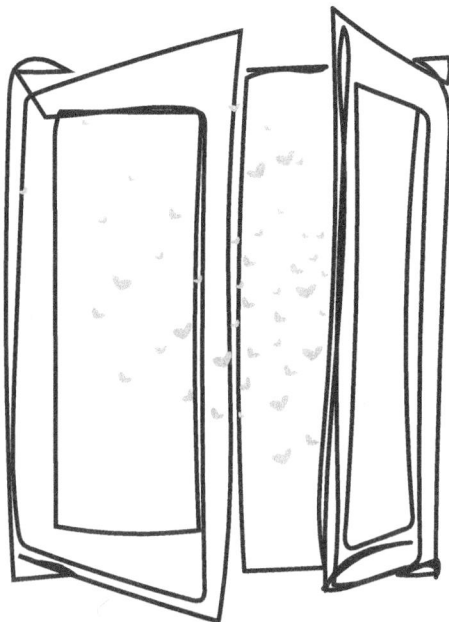

"Let your feelings be beautiful and belong to you.
But if you're sharing them, only share the beautiful ones."

46th message: THE PASSION OF THE SOUL AND AN OPEN WINDOW

Dear Sandra,

My angel, a lot in many things in this world are limited by fear. Fear of anything. The greatest **fear** is always born from not loving oneself. When someone is not happy with themselves, when they do not believe in themselves, and they are mistrustful and do not see the beautiful picture inside of themselves, they become timid and deathly afraid. Their will to be good withers. More and more, they are driven by dissatisfaction, guilt, and ugliness. They cannot escape their ego system, which is always dictated by fear. This fear is nothing more than an illusion, an illusion that maybe something better can be found, something better done, and be comforted by something from "outside". But within, they remain in a paradise of pointless moments of dissatisfaction that are transformed into fear of themselves and others, and it does not lead to a brighter tomorrow.

God's world doesn't know this, it does not know the feeling of fear, but only a beautiful feeling full of love that is as quiet as a tear! They do not need any greater fears or anything similar because they distance themselves from the thinking that love is no longer possible.

So, what to do in this situation? Start loving yourself. Become the one who accepts love for himself and is not spinning around in this circle of disappointment and doubts about themselves.

Do not accept the critiques of others, let it not even touch you, because you're not interested in that. This is a guidepost to begin differently. Otherwise, you will be blown away into the world of fear, which is nothing but the illusory state of the spirit. Relaxation in the most difficult moments is difficult to achieve, but you can breathe with relaxation and check how your heart can open up even more.

These are not the signals of the voice that are opening it, but the feelings. The feelings of joy, harmony, and beauty.

Grab them and take them in "the little heart of your heart" and let them soar into the skies. Look with your head into the sky and allow yourself to be what you are. The most beautiful, smartest, bravest, and wisest soul is the one that trusts in itself and in the system of guiding by emotion. Don't let the wagon with the fear of stress lead you away from the train. Rather serve yourself in a different environment with the most beautiful scenes of love areas, which you sing to yourself and those closest to you, strangers, and to me. The arias will announce deep or high, depending on how much your voice can manage. That is when you free yourself from the shackles of fear and feel the **passion of the soul.** Yes, the passion of the soul will drive you onward like a machine into the ever-greater non-illusory heights and dimensions, which will risk a little smaller incitement of fear with the heart in balance. Your heart will open up in balance as if it were an open window. Can you imagine it?

See the world through the eyes of a soldier who does not care that he will lose the battle. When the window fully opens, his heart opens up just enough to be open to love and beautiful things. It is a wonderful feeling. That is when the soul sings. But when it is in sync with the mind, amazing things begin to happen. The greatest creations, the greatest ideas, and the most beautiful things happen when the soul sings and the mind is at peace.

Your God.

"Let Light be the guide of your heart."

47th message: THE BOY'S STORY AND THE WISH-GRANTING FORMULA

Dear Sandra,

My angel, take this message into your notes and give it to the world.

What is given to a person to choose as he wishes? The wish, absence of a wish, bravery, the greatest invitation throughout all life to try and remain faithful to themselves and the desires they have?

There is no greater joy and no greater gift than to remain loyal to yourselves and, with that, serve others. That is when the soul is fulfilled by doing what it wants and for which it sings. When it sings, it does so out of love, and the mind and ego rest.

I remember a boy who had no mother and was put into foster care. His whole life, he was still joyous, happy, and never moaned, complained, or judged... He liked to help people, he loved his foster parents. He was a giant in the true sense of the word.

He was never unhappy; he didn't look for happiness outside of himself, but painted it within himself in his heart. My heart grew and grew. He was a strong person with many beautiful acts that he shared with others. When he was working from the heart, when his mind was working with beautiful thoughts and was open to all the love of this world, all of his wishes came true.

All his little wishes, and then those really big wishes. You know it's like this diagram:

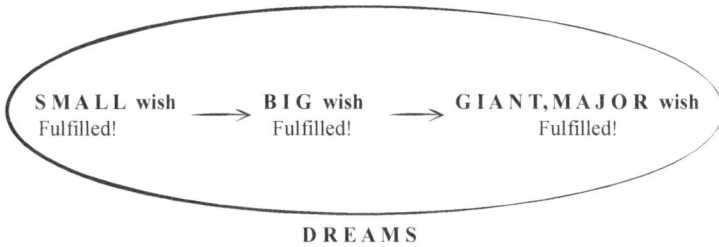

```
          SMALL wish  ──→  BIG wish  ──→  GIANT,MAJOR wish
          Fulfilled!       Fulfilled!     Fulfilled!

                          DREAMS
```

The dreams of this small, joyous person became REALITY. Whatever he wished, starting from the littlest wishes and up to those bigger ones, everything came true. He didn't doubt himself, he loved himself, he loved his mind and body, and he played music every day. He loved his family; he loved the whole world.

Through such unconditional love, he manifested every wish, every little tiny wish he had. He did it unknowingly. Those tiny little wishes came true each day, little by little, and the bigger ones in the shortest amount of time. His will and unconditional love he nurtured for himself and other people, living beings, nature, fellow man, cats, dogs, flowers, doves, and everything living and non-living on this planet, on this Earth, brought him joy and happiness, fulfilled him in a soulful sense, and brought everything this man desired, into his life.

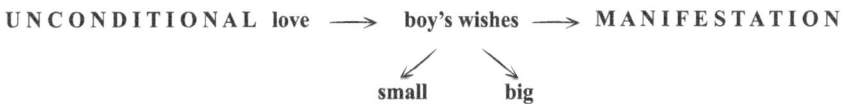

```
UNCONDITIONAL love  ──→  boy's wishes  ──→  MANIFESTATION
                              ↙    ↘
                          small    big
```

The boy's love was recognized by all. The vibration of his love reverberated far around and spread and warmed the love on every end of the world. It attracted a great amount of love, which the boy spread around even more.

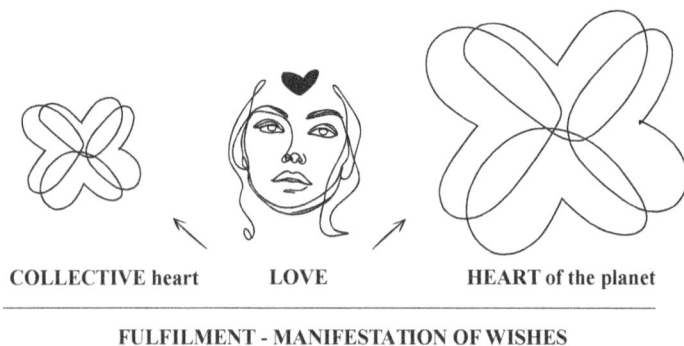

COLLECTIVE heart   LOVE   HEART of the planet

FULFILMENT - MANIFESTATION OF WISHES

The boy, in exchange for his love, did not expect anything; he only loved himself and **everything**, because he knew that everything is ONE, that we are all ONE. So, he walked this little Earth with an open heart, making true, manifesting all of his little and big wishes, and basking in the joy, wealth of money, prosperity of everything, beautiful relationships, harmony, and health.

But what would the story of the boy play out if he hadn't worked the way he did, if love hadn't played in his heart and his ego came out and knocked on the door of his mind and whispered to him that sometimes he must feel a little fear, that he doesn't have to love everyone, that he doesn't have to love money, that he must sometimes get sick, to argue with himself and his fellow villagers, that he has to sometimes hit someone and judge someone about this or that?

The story would be completely different. His little wishes, let alone his big wishes, would not manifest. Because the manifestation would not happen, he would be even more sad, unhappy, and downtrodden. He would do things that would derail his little wagon because he would be separated from the train.

Like this:

BOY'S little wish   **WISH**   **BIG WISH**
=   ∧   =
DOES NOT MANIFEST

This is how we can show the little story in reverse. We can also show it like this:

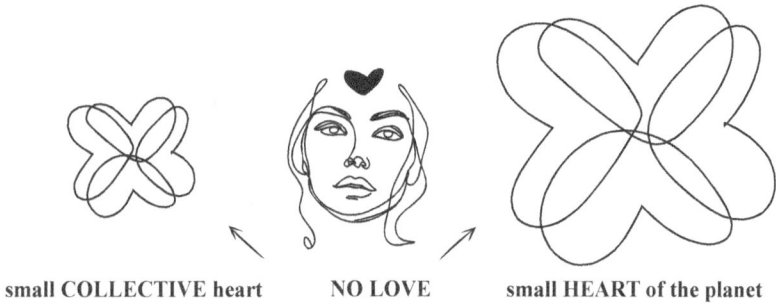

small COLLECTIVE heart   NO LOVE   small HEART of the planet

"UN-FULFILMENT" OF WISHES

So, my dear friends, stay who you are in your heart, true to yourself. That means that you do what you love and that you love yourself and love those things you love and not love those that others have, and to love others. That is the formula for fulfilling wishes. Good luck manifesting all your wishes, my dear friends!

Your God!

"You are the one to feel all the trash of the world. Make a world without trash."

48th message: LIVING TOGETHER ON THIS LITTLE EARTH

My dear Sandra,

My angel, let today's message be intended for the beauty of humanity, who knows that the Earth is the only place of their being. And what is the little Earth like today when looking at it from above, as I dwell in all of you and all the things that surround you? I am God and am **omnipresent**.

Do you know I am omnipresent? Some of you are already aware of this and others less so, but more and more of you are beginning to realize that I am somewhere around here, maybe around you, and maybe even inside you.

What will we say about this little Earth? That the coexistence of humans and other creatures should be beautiful and natural in a state of unconditional love. It's known that this is the human's home, and it's known that this is the home of the animals and other living creatures.

But this home is only temporary for my friends. Your karma follows you from your past lives, and you've brought it to this planet, and you'll take it into your next life when you get to your true **home**. Because when you die, you see your life on Earth as limited, as if you are only here for a short time.

However, only your body dies, while your soul or spirit actually travels back to its true home. Your life is eternal because your soul is immortal. Everything is energy. Your energy transforms into something else when it arrives back home, when it releases the body coat and ascends into another soulful life and a different soulful experience.

Your existence here on this little Earth interests me mainly because I wish to tell you how to most easily inhabit and cohabit in a limited time (and spatial) span on this little Earth. What do you do when your cohabitation with others on this little Earth becomes unbearable? Some do nothing. Others are looking for the guilty in others, and others still join environmental organizations to protect nature, the planet, and animals. Others are still happy with their life and what they have, while still others are somewhere between all four with a little of each. A mix of different living patterns.

Let's look at the ones that join every nature and animal conservation organization, and fight for the preservation of the planet – all the ecologically conscious people.

I applaud all who wish all the best for nature and all the animals. It's nice of you to put effort into preserving nature, the animals and plants, the forests, rivers, and seas. But your coming together to put things in order is not noteworthy, that will bring something to this world. It is a totality of negative energies and negative, low vibrations created to fight something.

My dear friends, the fight against something will always bring an even greater struggle into the energy field.

Advocate instead for energy that is at a higher vibration and supports you in all of your actions. If you advocate for a cleaner, more beautiful nature, you will contribute to peace, which will vibrationally strengthen you and will have visible results.

What about the other people who are indifferent and are beginning to become aware of the meaning of coexistence? These may correspond to a higher energy level that brings good, better results in terms of coexistence, but there are not many such instances, so they do not contribute much to coexistence.

Those who fill the *cauldron* of coexistence with love bring the most to this world. They give love and they receive it.

Those who do not care about anything aren't getting any energy in the coexistence space, not the energy that would harm, nor the one that would benefit. They are keeping the status quo, which is located somewhere between nowhere and barely noticeable.

The louder the rights of coexistence on this planet get, the more the energies will start to move. If you wish for more drinking water, you'll have to start appreciating it more, synchronizing yourself with the water, and you'll have to start putting it on a pedestal of the greatest good that brings the most life, because you are all practically living from it, and it is your source of life.

Energetically, this means that water, as the fundamental source of survival, is a highly appreciated good, which you should value and respect even more, and treat it in an energetically positive way. Its clarity, purity, and drinkability should send high vibrations through your veins, aligning you with the Earth's vibrations. That is how the most important coexistent living conditions and actions should be running.

Are we aware that we need to take care of the energy sources of all our coexisting conditions – they are getting depleted? I'm talking about oil, salt, water... All these need to be cared for in a way to maximize humanity and improve people, and in the context of an ever-expanding humanity. "Everything is in abundance", you will say. It's true, but the physical supplies of some materials and sources of life have been a little depleted on this little Earth.

We should care more about them until the supplies are balanced and humanity is happy in the long run. Take good care of nature and share unconditional love. Take good care of nature and share unconditional love everywhere so that coexistence on the little Earth will be beautiful and inspiring each day.

Your God.

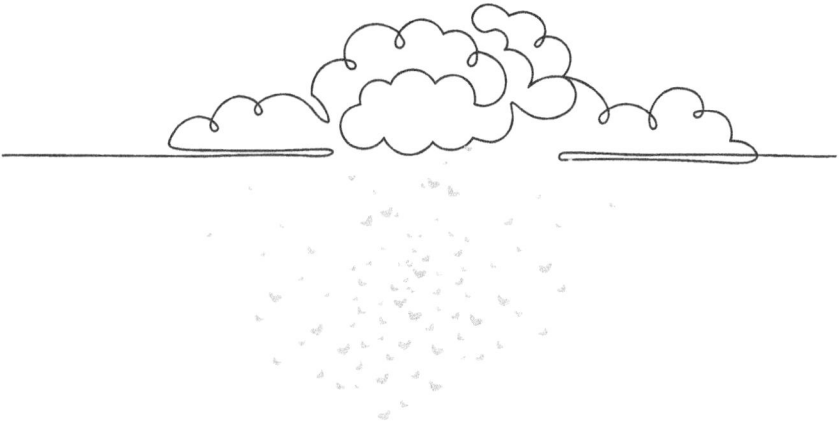

"Take care of what you have, be grateful, and you will have even
more. This is a rule."

49th message: SMALL MIRACLES FROM HEAVEN

Dear Sandra,

My angel, listen to me and bring today's message to the world. Let my message reach every single person on Earth.

What I will tell you today is a miracle. A miracle of what you can be and what you already are. You are the miracle of this world, my dear friends! I catch myself when I look at you and admire you, how some of you shine so divinely, and some of you less. You are a miracle from heaven, which you can have and catch every single moment in your life.

A miracle for you is something wonderful, unrepeatable, unique, something that doesn't happen day after day, and that happens incomprehensibly. Your amazement with the miracle is always great. You strive towards making every miracle happen. Sometimes you wish that a really big miracle would happen.

But what do you think is a **miracle**? Nothing like what you imagine it is.

Only your brain thinks a miracle is something that's rarely possible, something that rarely happens, and even then, only to certain people, but what I'm trying to tell you is that for you, my dear friends, every day can be a giant miracle. Even while you're walking on this little Earth and you're looking around for a miracle to happen. You must experience this somehow in the higher vibrations with higher energies. Perhaps you think that a miracle happened to you because you've won a million dollars on the lottery, but that was no miracle, but only the fruit of your manifestation, faith, and trust in whatever you wanted.

Do you think you are a miracle? Yes, perhaps in some way because we chose you specifically to miraculously incarnate into your divine body on Earth, but life is not a miracle. A miracle is everything you cannot explain or imagine that originates from the divine and the energy of the divine. You come from the divine and divine energy, as do your parents and your mobile applications on your phone, your food and drink, everything – everything originates from me, I am present everywhere and in everything. Then it is not a miracle, my dear friends.

Miracles happen to you because you think and feel that way. I cannot tell you how much I wish for you all to be better attuned to the higher vibrations, the vibrations of the divine, which are up here, and you can take it whenever you want. When you, for example, go to the store and buy something, and they give you a discount, are you happy about that? Of course, you are because you're saving money. You're happy and strong, and it seems great that the seller sold it for a dollar.

But this is not a miracle, it is an action that you take for granted. You don't see that as a miracle, do you? But why don't you see that as a miracle? You could. The seller gave you a discount, and you miraculously saved money… So, this is something that is self-evident and doesn't belong under the term *miracle*. Because under the term "miracle" you imagine something unrepeatable, something glorious, something that doesn't happen every day, and maybe God rewarded you… Miraculously…

Let's say that the discount could be a miracle – could you perceive it that way? What if someone ties your shoes? Is it a miracle or something that you take for granted every day, for which you can be grateful? What about when a brother, a classmate, a beautiful boy or girl, or a stranger you've just met hugs you? Maybe all that is a miracle. Or is it? "Oh no, those are not miracles", you'll say, "that's just what happens when someone hugs you or gives you a discount... Not all those are miracles, it's just reality that happens."

Well then, my dear friends, let's turn these into miracles, small miracles for which we can be grateful every single day. Those little joys of happiness bring us gratitude, fortune, hope for the future, and love.

Let these small, little moments that brighten up your days be something that you call a "miracle". These are not miracles, I assure you, but you classify them as miracles, small miracles that happen to you all the time every day. When someone gives up their seat on the bus, when they give you a friendly look, when someone truly loves you, when you are truly loved, when you go somewhere and offer you a drink, or when you are simply happy... Then my dear friends take all these tiny wonders.

Wonders that awaken within you the feeling of gratitude and pleasantness, feelings which make your energy even more beautiful and approach the divine. If this is good and is a remedy for you, then please, from this day onward, take this life as a joyous miracle you're happy for. Walk around with an open heart, grabbing it by the horns in all its might and greatness because the power is within you, my dear friends. I will talk to you about power next time, let my dear angel Sandra remind me of it.

I say, let your moments on Earth be miraculously miraculous, let them bring you divine and beautiful feelings even though they are no real miracles. But because this miracle is something fine and positive, something that elevates you to a higher plane of energy, imagine everything as a miracle, and your life will be more beautiful. Your life will be fulfilled in the divine way only love can manage. Again, we find ourselves with love.

Even the miracles that seem like miracles should be for you a priceless love that heals. From within. Not from without.

Your God.

"There is no rule for LOVE. It just is."

50ᵗʰ message: POWER IS WITHIN YOU WHEN YOU FEEL LOVE

Dear Sandra,

My dear angel! Everything that is connected to power is us. We have within us immeasurable **power** that can move mountains, manifest the known and unknown, and lower us into depths and dimensions the likes of which the human body cannot imagine.

Let me tell you about your real power. It is a mix of actions, a mix of insane possibilities that dwell within you. It is immeasurable and invisible. Perhaps you don't see the power within yourself, but you must see it, you must see it today. I'm not talking about physical power, I'm talking about your spiritual power, a power from which you can create everything and have everything you've ever imagined.

The power is within you, it is a tiny little spark just waiting to be ignited. Like a fire that you start. Try it, my dear friends, it is a magnificent act. You have the power to be completely healthy and beautiful, and in beautiful relationships, you have the power to behave well and to have all the money in the world if you wish it… All the plenty you can have if you want it.

What worries me the most sometimes is that you **are not using it**. You're not using all your potential, so you can have all that you want. You have the power within yourself to be healthy. To be happy. Write "Power" in capital letters. Power is all-powerful; try using it a little and, at least for a moment, feel it. It is within you, nowhere else. Don't look for it outside of yourself, in other people, in different situations, on the other side of the world... Your power isn't there, my dear friends. Your power is inside of you, as is your heart.

Put in some effort as if you are starting to build a house. First, you need a plan, then the materials, and next, the workers who will build the house according to the plan. That is how your power works.

Go on, tell yourself what you want, plan what you want... then tell yourself to make these wishes come true (let us say you wish to lose some weight or gain some weight so you can be healthy or you wish to have more money), then find the power within yourself to make these actions happen.

The power is IN YOU!

Power is my dear friends like a construction company that builds your house. This is how it is in your life too – to manifest something into your life and to be fulfilled in your life in every area of your life, you use POWER. You use it as if you wish to build a house. It is no different.

Where do you find the source of your power? Deep within yourself. Draw it out with your thinking about the greatest power on Earth and bring it to the surface from the depths of your spirit.

Wait for it to climb to the surface, then grab it and use it. Be strong in the sense of working positively with the help of power, which is nothing more than AN ILLUSION, which will bring to you all the good things in life and work like a hot spring that never goes out.

Let's go even further. What do you think power is? Is it something you sense? Is it something you feel? You do, of course, you do. But when do you feel it? When you are in a state of LOVE. Only then do you feel the POWER inside yourself. You will be hard-pressed to find it before. Why? Because when love is not in you, it's not there!

You never have power when you do not act out of love. When you don't act out of love (capitalize it), you are POWERLESS. You can't find your *construction company* to help you build the house. It's the same with power.

Even though it's an illusion, my dear friends, pure illusion = POWER.

POWER = PURE ILLUSION

You won't find power when you are in a state of POWERLESSNESS! You won't be able to find it because it's just not there. So, my dear friends, go, love, work out of love, make a collective spiral, contribute to it, and your power will be within you always, when it is I'm with you too.

Your God.

"You won't expend yourself because of money.
Money will expend your thoughts if you wish too much for it."

51ˢᵗ message: BEINGS WHO SPREAD LOVE ON THIS LITTLE EARTH

Dear Sandra,

My angel, let me tell you something about the glorious, great gods worshiped by your ancestors in Athens and in Rome. Let me also tell you about the historical personalities you learn in your history classes. Today, these gods, like me, are ascended creatures in the kingdom of Heaven, beings without bodies, only souls. Jesus, Athena, Zeus, Buda, Krishna, Moses, Saint Germain – all of these that I list – are ascended beings who sit at my side today, but once they were the light on this planet, they were masters.

There are many beings like this on Earth that also spread the light of divinity, and you were sent to raise the energy of people, living beings, and the planet. There are many of you, and you are here too, my dear Sandra, my angel that spreads my word, that is the word of love. You were picked by Jesus; you are Jesus's angel. An angel incarnate that will shine and share its divinity and whiteness forward. Maybe put this in the introduction itself. I will tell you what you should put into the introduction of this book, you'll release (the text dictated to me was put into the introduction of this book).

Your God.

"Go into nature, the charm of love is always present there."

52ⁿᵈ message: KEEP INFATUATION FOR LIFE AND FOR YOURSELF

Dear Sandra,

My angel, today your hands are my mouth. What I say and communicate, you write down. Let my messages be your writings from me to the world.

Now we're going to direct ourselves to something that people love very much: **infatuation**. Who doesn't want to feel this strong, powerful, and beautiful emotion at least once in their life? In these moments, your emotions are drenched with powerful feelings that take you to unknown heights and make you significantly unpredictable. You don't know how to behave, what to eat, how to live... These powerful energies that hit you in times of infatuation, my friends, your head, body, mind, and spirit are surely singing then, but somehow your soul is not directed towards its mission and whatever it wants.

Many of you have already felt this terrifyingly beautiful feeling. Why do you all say it is so beautiful? Because that is when you feel the special energy that transports you into a completely new and unknown world. But can your infatuation last forever? It can, but souls that can drag infatuation into forever are rare.

I am not even talking about the relationship between two partners, I'm talking about infatuation in general. Infatuation with yourself, children, animals, trips, absolutely everything you can become infatuated with.

When you are, for example, infatuated with your partner, my friends, you are in some kind of highly mentally dependent state that leads you to other energetic heights and energies. I can't tell you how funny it is to me when infatuation turns into its last phase, a phase of addiction. Because of this, your mentality sometimes suffers.

Yes, you heard that right, suffers my dear friends. It is a feeling that causes suffering because, in this period, the heart is being tested, and the body is under stress. The body releases huge amounts of new hormonal reactions, which are not only new to your body and mind but are also very intense. And your intensive energy transforms into intensive actions.

At those times you scream, sleep restlessly, change your clothes, can't eat, go dig a hole, feel sorry for yourself, don't like yourself, and can fall into delirium...all of this leads you into states of dependency, which energetically don't last long because your body, mind, and soul can't handle it anymore.

Of course, infatuation is at a certain point also the feeling of happiness, harmony, and beauty; while the feeling of beauty is at a certain point love itself, but this emotion itself is too strong based on the current experience, and oftentimes actions don't equate to more love.

When you are terribly in love, you, my friends, are also terribly vulnerable. Unable to judge right from wrong, your head can slip into certain fears, insecurities, and other thought patterns that don't fit you and are not love.

So, I tell you that states like these quickly lead to unbalanced extreme situations that cause indifference and *unlove*. The greater risk you take due to your infatuation, the more your soul will be vulnerable. In a vulnerable state, people very rarely make good decisions. Because these decisions are not good, these things end together with the story of infatuation. Before you decide to fall in love madly, take a step back for a moment, open your eyes, and say you love yourself first.

Don't throw Cupid's arrow everywhere so it doesn't hit a soul. The soul won't last long and will wave "a white flag" in defeat, letting you know that it's over.

Everything you need to know about infatuation is that it is an emotion that, at a certain point, reaches love, but only for a short amount of time. When it exceeds it, love turns to *unlove*. This is why the aftermath of love is so painful and not committed to love. Every marriage or partnership between two people that starts with love and giant butterflies in the stomach ends with some kind of reconciliation, which ends the state of love, returns it to its initial state, or continues without infatuation.

Infatuation is such a powerful emotion, but I'm trying to tell you that you should not cling to it for long, because in the end, it will not bring you what you want, a long-term emotional mental state, but post festum maybe just a sober relationship without the obvious infatuation.

May each of your days begin in a way that is worth being in love first with yourself, your life, and not others. When you, with your infatuated eyes, without excessive trembling at fearful thoughts, come to the fact that you love yourself the most and that your infatuation with yourself means healthy self-confidence and self-respect, that will also bring love for others. But keep infatuation for yourself and for life. Every relationship, with a partner or any other relationship, should be the logical continuation of loving yourself.

Your God.

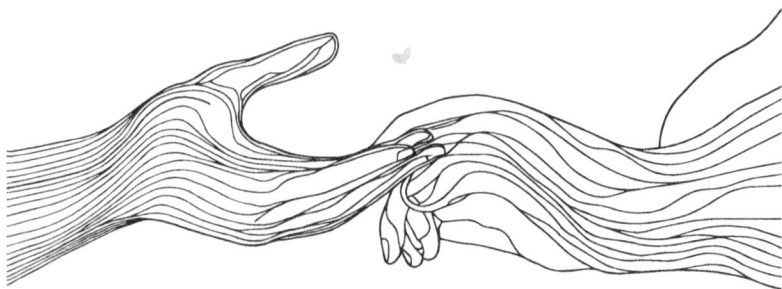

"Keep looking forward. Your past holds nothing
because it is not there."

53rd message: HAPPY IS THE ONE WHOSE HAPPINESS DOES NOT "HANG AROUND HIS NECK", BUT RESIDES WITHIN HIM

Joyful is your heart that feels my love. You walk around with an open heart, open to absolutely everything. Everything you wish for, you get. Children love you; parents respect you; your coworkers are proud of you and want to be like you, and the *greatest living* in this world seems like something magical.

Every moment holds the magic that you recognize. Even the walls in your room seem magical to you, the slippers on your wife, the beautiful hair on your colleague, and the most beautiful muscles on a bodybuilder. All the little things barely noticed by the eye seem magical because you are magical yourself.

Your charisma is amazing, and everyone wants to be like you because you exude this energy. They want to make love with you, walk with you, eat the same food as you, hang out with you, and do everything with you. People notice this. It's energy. Even other living beings like animals notice it.

They feel exactly what you're giving off, my dear friend. Your vibrations are like a cable that everyone wants to pull towards themselves and put into their plug and charge themselves. But my dear friend, that can only happen when you are with me and my angels, when your heart is open, listening, and receiving the energy of the divine you're giving it.

Happy is the one whose happiness does not "hang around his neck" but resides within him. He is aware of his happy side, and even the ozone seems infinitely beautiful. Hmm, what is ozone anyway, where is it, and what does it look like?

But he knows that that *dear person* feels it that way.

It's a mistake to think that happiness just comes and goes on its own. It doesn't come and go. It can always be here, sitting inside of you, and you decide to lure it out of yourself. You can't look for it somewhere else, in other people, other places or any other place because it doesn't exist there for you and you'll never find it there.

That is all about the happiness that always accompanies you when you have an open heart and a divine, energetically aligned soul, filled with happiness and situations that do not long for happiness to be sought elsewhere.

Your God.

"The future is in your hands. Grab the key
to the most beautiful door."

54th message: EVERYTHING IS INSIDE YOU – WITHIN YOU, AND YOU ALONE. EVEN JOY

Dear Sandra,

My angel, let me say something about joy today.

What makes you happy, my dear friends? Maybe your cat that purrs around your feet, maybe your beautiful baby whose teeth you can see growing, maybe your coworker that brings you your coffee in the morning, maybe your beautiful body when you look into the mirror, maybe your heart that's beating healthily and leading you into a wonderful life with an open heart. Is this joy to you? It is. For many of you, the things I just listed are joy. But joy is much more than that, my dear friends.

JOY is **in** you
⟶

NOT in what is **around you**

When you are in a joyous feeling, you glow, love, and are loved. That's why you love to say that your soul is joyous. But my dear friends, I wish to tell you that you should not seek joy or happiness outside of yourself, but look for it inside, because the thing that gives you the feeling of joy you love so much and which you give to others is inside of you. Joyous is the heart when it is open; when you investigate the world with beautiful purple eyes and glasses, because then your mind, body, and soul take you into joyous emotions. If you are not joyous yourself and you look for joy in your cat, husband, or other people, or in general in the outside world, you will not easily feel or experience this joy. Joy, my friends, comes from within, as does your happiness. That is what I'm telling you. Everything is inside you. Everything is within you. Within and only in you.

When you feel the joy inside yourself, you're taken over by the emotion, you feel the emotion, you have the emotion. Of course, your dog, kitty cat, or your husband can give you feelings of joy, which you will feel as a higher vibration. It can elevate you to a better and higher level of energy when you catch yourself thinking negatively or are in an energetically very low state.

When this happens, these outside factors can accelerate the beating of your heart and open it in a way to raise your vibration. That is a very good way to move yourself from a lower vibration to a higher vibration. People vibrate all the time, which I will talk about more next time (let Sandra, my angel, remind me of this next time), because the vibration you give off is very important. You see, energetically, you either do or do not align with the divine. So, you are either in harmony or disharmony with the divine. Whether you are in a state of love or not.

I want to give you advice: whenever you catch yourself on low vibrations and you are drenched in fear, reluctance, and worry, when you are cranky and your day just isn't flowing, and you are not "in the feeling" of happiness and joy - try **to raise your vibration.**

Raising your vibration is very simple. You pet your dog or a cat, cuddle with your husband, or do something that will raise your vibration. A hug from your loving husband or partner will most definitely feel good and raise your vibration. When you catch yourself that you are cranky or afraid, become aware of this feeling and your lower vibration and tell yourself: "Hey, time to raise my vibration to the next level!"

And then do something that will bring you to the next level. Go in front of a mirror, hug yourself, and tell yourself how much you love yourself, how beautiful you are, and experience that for a few moments.

Experience this feeling, which will at the same time raise your vibration and help realign yourself with divine energy, with me, because it will open your heart. Then you will feel this feeling of happiness and joy inside yourself. Happiness and joy are basically the same feelings – we can say that by the feeling of them, they are the same emotions and feelings, except that joy is a broader term, which I understand as lasting longer. And even your joy, of course, except that joy may come and go exactly because of your everyday perceptions, perceptions of the environment, and outside factors, which love to take your moments of joy away. So, you jump up and down the energy vibration scale.

Be in your element, or in other words, be with me, be coordinated with divine energy, and your joy will sing within you. Do not look for it in new shoes or new material things; look for it inside yourself.

Your God.

"The heart is the one when it's beating in the rhythm of love."

55th message: LOVE EVERYTHING AND EVERYONE. WE ARE ALL ONE

Dear Sandra,

My Angel, for the ending, let me tell you this: go and take everything I've told you in one month and take my messages with this divine book, the book of love to the world and every living person. Let them read it with an open heart, and may their life be always more fulfilled. Let every word in this book heal them, let it work on them as medicine, as a water kefir you made yourself today for yourself and your family.

May you be watched over by your loved ones, your angels, your spiritual guides, incarnated angels, and all the divine and heavenly beings from the kingdom of God; may they lead you down the path that is best for you and is in line with your life's purpose.

I, God, am also with you, watching you, protecting you, and simply loving you.

Share your love forward to:

1.   YOURSELF

2.   OTHERS

3.   EVERYTHING YOU HAVE, SEE, HEAR, OR TOUCH

4.   LOVE EVERYONE AND EVERYTHING.
     WE ARE ALL ONE

Let this be the first rule in your physical life. Let it guide you down the path you're walking down. Don't try to find yourself anywhere else but inside yourself, and be tightly connected to my divine energy. I tell you this through all the messages in the book because this is the main thread, the essence, the heart of this booklet, which you are reading thanks to our angel Sandra. I want to call her Angela. Because Sandra is our angel. I've chosen her to spread my word and my teaching across the world. That is why I now call her Angela.

Dear Sandra, my dear angel, let your name be divine today, and your second name be Angela.

That is how I see you and how I call you. And when I call you, my dear Angela, you are sheltered by me. I am somewhere close by, "breathing down your collar", on your left like a guardian angel.

Your book is the book of LOVE. You wrote it, dear Angela. Let every human on this planet read it, because every letter will work on them spiritually and medicinally. Every single letter that they read will imprint itself into the memory of the human mind and "reprogram" their mind. The mind will become flexible like an elastic that you can tighten, and so his thinking will be the same as light.

This is what I wanted to say to each and every person on the *little Earth*. When I talk about a topic that seems a little *frozen* or different from the ones you are used to, my dear friends, many will laugh, then think about it, and throw the book away, or take it as real medicine. Like a potion, it will fill him with the intoxicating energy of love and become the *child of love* that was sent to this little Earth. But the childlike playfulness, unconditional love, and everything get lost somewhere along the way and are covered up by habits, patterns, systems, and everything surrounding a person that takes them away from the intoxication of love. A child who grows up into an adult often doesn't feel the intoxication of love. That is how it is with most of adults.

So my dear friends, drink all of my words from this book and let them take you into a new, different energy source where you will again connect to your divine light.

Your God.

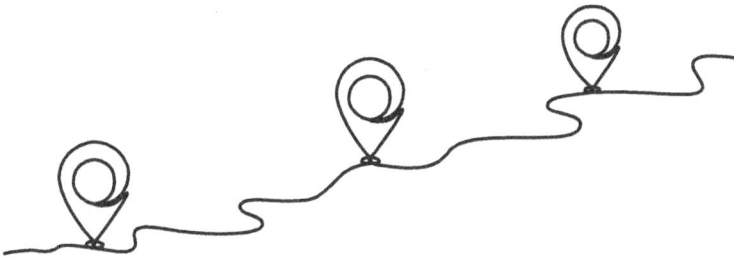

"Why are you asking yourself what will be,
when you have to focus on what is."

56th message: THE PATH ON THE EARTH
OR THE LINE OF LIFE

Dear Angela,

Beyond the invisible, everything begins. Beyond the invisible, everything lasts forever, and beyond the invisible, **everything is**. Eternal, infinite, with boundless LOVE.

When, from beyond the visible in flies a spark of the divine and ignites, **someone** may incarnate in this material world. The spark in the mother's womb becomes a human embryo and is born as a baby, and then grows into an adult. That is how the journey starts for them. The path I'm describing goes like this:

**SPARK - the BABY
embryo in mother's womb**

BABY

baby, child, ADULT

 P A T H

no beginning   it's just THE PATH on the "little" Earth   no end

You see the line that is limited by two people, the baby on

the left and the adult on the right? You think that these two are the beginning of life when you are born and you incarnate into your little body on Earth, and the end of your physical life on this Earth, death.

NO, no, no, no!!! There is no beginning or end here. The line is just THE PATH. Write it in all capital letters, it is just THE PATH.

A path that never starts and never ends. Your body is born, your body dies. Only the body! Do you understand me? Your spirit, your soul never! You never die, pass away, or disappear. My dear friends, you just walk the line, this path from the left to the right.

And in this book, I'm giving you instructions (that my dear Angela is writing down) on how to most easily walk the path in plenty, fortune, happiness, harmony, and JOY, good relationships, and financial plenty. Here I give you instructions on *how to have this path in your possession* so that life comes to you. And what is the thing that makes the path beautiful, clean, and filled to the brim with your life's purpose, to make true that which our souls had already agreed to before you arrived here? It's love. Only love will truly, impeccably, beautifully, cleanly, and joyfully lead you down this path.

Love is the only guide on the path of life.

Your God.

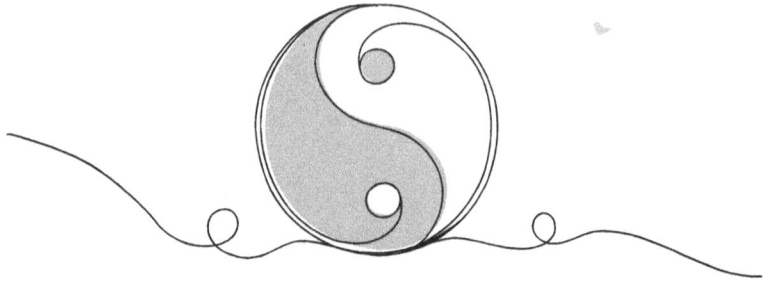

"Your paths are filled with glamor when you are beautiful."

57th message: EXCESSIVE EMOTIVENESS

Dear Angela,

Take this message far too. Let me tell you something about excessiveness, what it actually means, and how people should act when they become excessive with their emotions, relationships, money, happiness, and harmony.

When a person is wasteful and excessive with their strong emotions, they are under the strong influence of their thoughts and mentality. That is when the emotions are working. Emotions are thought. We have emotions when we think. These emotions can be **positive** (+) or **negative** (-). When you excessively emote your negative emotions, that means you are not in alignment with me.

Exaggerated fear, exaggerated anger, and all exaggerated, almost manic, emotions lead you into very low vibrations. When you start to excessively emote with them, you are trapped. Trapped in a wheel of despair, great sadness, ugliness, and unhappiness.

Excessive **emotiveness** (-)   ↓   **VIBRATIONS** fear, despair, discomfort

When you excessively feel positive emotions, it means that your thoughts are good and very positive. When your thinking reacts to your very positive, beautiful thoughts with good and very intense positive emotions, this is actually very good, as you are transitioning to good vibrations and responding in a good, beautiful, positive, compassionate, and loving way.

Excessive **emotiveness** (+)   ↑   **VIBRATIONS** LOVE ♥

When you again excessively emote other things, let's say money, it's not bad. People think it is bad for them to spend money. You can't feel bad if you're excessively spending money. Money is just energy. Money can again bring positive or negative connotations with your emotions when it comes to excess. When you think you are spending too much and think you don't have it, or think you're going to be running out, you're sinking into the world of low energy and low vibrations. And in reverse, when you know you are doing good with your money, that is positive for you, you are turning towards the higher vibration. The diagram could be similar in terms of emoting and connection with your emotional scale, and emoting and creating or emitting your own vibrations, even when spending money.

Emotions reflect your thoughts, nothing more. It is all mental. If you allow your thoughts to bring you to beautiful, comfortable moments, you will be in a great place with your emotions.

The reverse is also true. If your thoughts are always negative, then your emotions are going to be negative as well. That is how your mentality works. Excessively spreading different types of thoughts means nothing different than spreading different types of (positive or negative) emotions.

The emotions you spread out negatively or positively take you on the scale of vibrations (of good and positive energy), something like this:

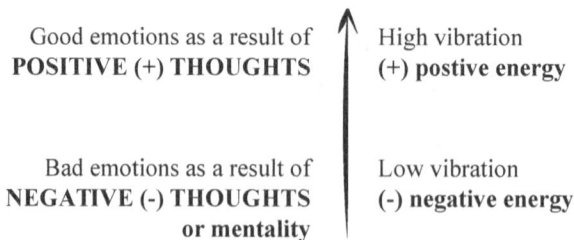

Good emotions as a result of **POSITIVE (+) THOUGHTS** ↑ High vibration (+) **postive energy**

Bad emotions as a result of **NEGATIVE (-) THOUGHTS or mentality** Low vibration (-) **negative energy**

You probably already know very well what good and bad thoughts and feelings are for you. If your boss at work makes you angry first thing in the morning, you're probably pretty angry, and your emotions are somewhere on the bottom of the scale. If you respond to the boss's anger with a smile, with patience, if you go into the day with optimism, no matter the circumstances that are part of your life, you are somewhere towards the top of the scale.

Your emotions are positive (+), you are calm, and thinking positively. And so you move up and down the scale all day. And in the end, this is how your day looks:

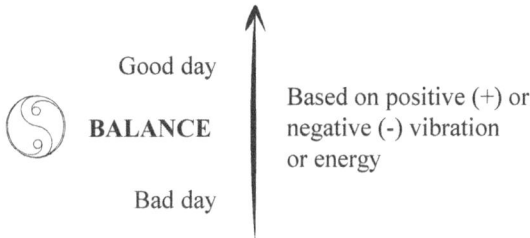

Good day

BALANCE

Based on positive (+) or negative (-) vibration or energy

Bad day

You know, my dear friends, there will always be outside factors that will discourage you from positive thoughts and positive energy. That is when you catch them and close your eyes, as I already explained. Let this be the moment you begin to realize your bad and negative emotions and thoughts, and you can try to raise your low vibration in a way that is closest to you. Will you pet your puppy, dance to your favorite music, hug someone… Then your vibration will spirally jump up the scale of energy and vibrations.

At that point, you will be aligned with me and with divine love, and you will again jump up the scale to the level of good energy.

Everything in life swings, even you and your energy and your vibration, because everything is energy, everything is one vibration.

The most important thing is that you become aware of where you are – up above or down below... If you are below, try and get into balance. That will bring you closer to me.

Everything is in balance, so veering down doesn't mean good energy, and it's important that you are aware when you're veering off and try to get yourself into balance as much as you can on the higher energies and frequencies. That is where I am. When you get up here, you are with me. For that, you only need love, and once you have it, you fly to me.

Your God.

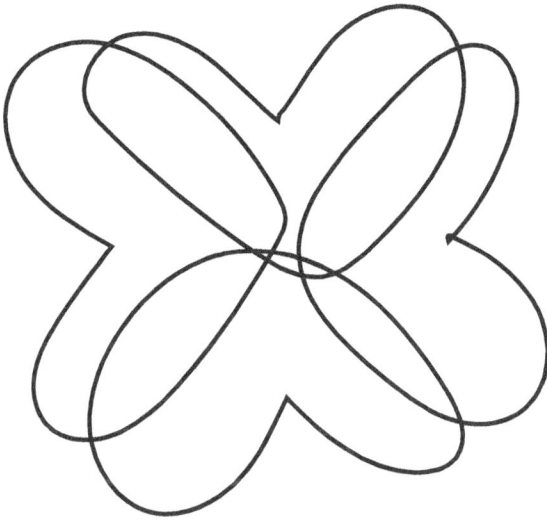

"You make the sun move where your beauty resides."

7th October 2019

58th message: LOVE IS EVERYTHING

Dear Angela S.,

Your writing is my blessing. Give it to people tomorrow in the form of a book. Let them start reading what I have to say. This moment will be just between us, and let's focus on another beautiful message.

Let me tell you another thing about love. I can't get past it, no, I can't get past it, I can't help myself without talking about it all the time. Talking about its beauty, its primacy, and where it comes from. Everything you see, everything you touch, and everything you hear is the product of pure, endless love that never runs out. It is always here and now. Not in the past and not in the future. It is always found in a form that you cannot see or touch and can only feel when you feel all other feelings, both positive and negative.

Why am I telling you again about love that comes from me and is embodied in you? Why am I repeating this so many times?

Love = EVERYTHING

This is a formula. A miraculous formula, if you will. Like a magical, fragrant, intoxicating, indescribably beautiful elixir in which everything begins and ends. Within are all the ingredients that all of you are looking for. Look at this pitcher now, this cup that contains the drug called love.

Do you see it? Do you see the magical, intoxicating cup? It's the cup that is filled with love, and within it is the drug of love.

The ingredients for this drug are:

- kind words
- good actions
- tenderness
- kisses
- hugs
- light, brightness

- goodness
- beauty
- harmony
- compassion
- empathy
- joy

- happiness
- grace
- warmth
- kind thoughts
- calm
- EVERYTHING

You see I listed some of the ingredients of Love! I can't list all of them, there are many because love = ALL.

Love = EVERYTHING

Let this book start this way, my dear Angela. At the start and at the end, write that LOVE IS EVERYTHING.

"EVERYTHING" means that it is everything we have, and it is everything you see on Earth, and is in a material state (my dear friends, you always like seeing something tangible). It is within everything. Everything started with love. Everything. Even you, my dear friends. Without love, you would not exist.

Unconditional, divine love creates a spark and ignites it – that is how you were created, I already told you this. When you spread love and your soul grows and develops in this vast universe. This is when you also develop and grow together with your soul part. That is the essence of our story of us and you. Of all of us. It is the essence of the universe. I, God the Creator, and you here on this little Earth, who can only come from Love. It drives you forward, moves you, it manifests through allowing and expanding the soul and divine energy.

The soul part cannot expand if there is no love inside of you. It doesn't move forward, and it does not expand, and neither do you. So quickly look into the cup and take from it all of the ingredients of love and tune yourself back to love as much as you've moved away from it. That is a rule, the one and only.

Tell yourself loudly that all of the ingredients are good and you will drink them every day, every single day, even if you sometimes don't see the cup or you think it's empty. It is never empty, never! Just try to see it with all of your ingredients together and drink it!

There is no other way. You add salt and pepper to your soup, right? In the same way, add all of the ingredients of love into your daily life so you can work and move forward. What I'm telling you is very important.

Angela S. is writing what you're reading. Read everything, every single word, because Angela S. was chosen to offer you this cup for you to see. Angela S. was chosen to put this cup on your kitchen table every day. All you have to do is take it and drink the intoxicating elixir of love.

P.S.: Angela S. is just your angel who helps you when you ask for it. She will hear you. And when she does, she will *place a cup in your kitchen*. **Imaginary cup**! Because the cup with all the ingredients of love is on the kitchen counter all the time, you just can't see it because you've distanced yourself. So, Angela S. comes and brings you the cup every time you pray for it and ask for it.

She is always with you. Even in this book. She will give it to you, my dear friends. Be Godly and with Love.

Your God.

"The loudness of your heart is conditioned by the light
and love for yourself."

59th message: MESSAGE OF THE ANGELS

Dear Angela, for the end!

Walk the path standing straight, raised up high in your happiness, joy, fulfillment, and PLENTY, and let life serve you.

Everything you wish for - manifest as I've taught you. The formula for manifestation is not complicated. Just allow yourself and be in the spirit of allowing it - allowing yourself to love yourself and to love. Search for the positive in life - positivity leads you to the perpetual depths of love, which enable contact with oneself, with your *head*, and enable your soul connection. Remain constantly in the state of ALLOWING. Everything you wish for - manifest. Manifestation is beautiful, and it is not a miracle if you are in a state of allowing.

Allow yourself to love and be loved, allow yourself to have money and to live in financial abundance, allow yourself great relationships, and allow yourself to be fulfilled in a business sense. Allow yourself to be perfect in every area of your life. You can only allow this when you are guided by LOVE.

Health – your health does not depend on outside factors, but on your physical balance. If you do not allow balance, you allow disease. If you are not in balance with yourself, you cannot have beautiful relationships. After all, you do not allow others to love you because you do not love yourself. You don't love because you can't, because you don't love yourself. You don't have money because you do not allow it, but you allow poverty and scarcity.

My dear friends, ALLOW and everything comes to you.

Life comes to you.

Your God.

9th October 2019

Angelic message

Our planet is on the edge of a fundamental change. The planet and the people on this little Earth are exposed and compelled to begin raising the vibration of the planet and of the people.

People need to start raising their vibration and connect again with everything that is, with divine energy. The planet has been looted and impoverished. A lot of damage has already been done, so it needs to be fixed.

This little Earth is a planet that is part of this boundless universe and of the divine expanse, and the low vibrations it emits have already started to affect the universe. That is why we Angels – God's right and left hand, if you will – are here to help raise the collective consciousness of this Earth and of the people on it.

This is already happening, and it must happen; otherwise, the planet will no longer be inhabitable. That is why you, Sandra, are also our light. You can use this book to spread consciousness among people on this planet, and with your healing help, raise the vibration inside people. All who are unable to raise their vibration in sequence and alignment with the rising vibration of the Earth will have a hard time living on this energetic level.

So, Sandra, with this book, heal as many people as you can and give them the power to raise their vibration so they can lift themselves into the light, the light from where they came from.

Amen.

FINAL WORD

Even as a little girl, I knew there was more beyond the visible. Something bigger and greater than us people and this little Earth. Something magical. Some mighty, magical force that encompasses everything, orders everything, and is credited with everything in the universe. God.

This invisible divine force tapped my shoulder and whispered to me to follow its dictation, to write this book and give it to you to read. To be frank, initially, I had no idea what I was supposed to be writing about.

The voice that kept talking to me and whispering to me to start to write became more and more intense every day, and even relentless at times. It wouldn't leave me alone. It was the voice of God. Exactly 30 days, the voice of God gently urged me with his angel and whispered to me words that I wrote down on paper. He even suggested the name of the book. He said that I'm writing a Book of Healing, a book of Love.

I wrote this book for all those who wish to become masters of their energies and, with the help of divine teachings, attach themselves to the loving system of help (God calls this healing). So healed, you will realize that life on this Earth can be quite glorious. Are you ready, dear friend, for this book to heal you and for your real life's work to begin?"

The energy to heal the world can only be obtained through love. That is the message of this book. This force – Love, God – found me to channel this message to the world.

Love is the self-healing energy. Love is God, and God is Love.

This entire text, all the letters, words, and sentences, is healing because the book is written in the Holy Spirit through the Eye of God. Healing divine energy flows through every letter. This book contains energy, it contains Love. It carries a teaching, a teaching about Love that may never dry up. And who, my friend, can give you better advice for living on this Earth than the Source of it all? No one. Not the therapist, doctor, healer, …

Everyone should read this book because as you read these words, every person will become a little bit more enlightened, *clean*, and healthy. So says the Source …

Angel S.

About the author

Sandra Angel Nešić, is a mother, a mentor, a friend ... a force of Nature, and also holds a Master's degree in Political Science.

She likes to inspire people and do good things in the world. She sees people and inspires them to believe in themselves at least as much as she believes in them; she motivates and encourages people to do more, be more, and have more.

She is courageous, and she trusts in her strength to create something good and beautiful for everyone in this life, which is why she also started writing this book. With it, she leaves her legacy, staying firm in her moral convictions and not shying away from challenges.

Her life motto: where there's a will, there's a way.

This book is her debut.

Let's get in touch on social media - I would like to hear how the messages in this book touched you.

You can always find me...

... on Instagram @**sandranesicx**

or visit my web page: **isana.si**

- there is no end -

www.ingramcontent.com/pod-product-compliance
Lightning Source LLC
LaVergne TN
LVHW051359080426
835508LV00022B/2896